INSIGHT *Pocket* GUIDES

BRITTANY

Written and Presented by **Nigel Tisdall**

Nigel Tisdall

INSIGHT
Pocket
GUIDES

Insight Pocket Guide:

BRITTANY

Directed by
Hans Höfer

Managing Editor
Andrew Eames

Photography by
Roger Hilton

Design Concept by
V. Barl

Design by
Karen Hoisington

© 1993 APA Publications (HK) Ltd

All Rights Reserved

Printed in Singapore by
Höfer Press (Pte) Ltd
Fax: 65-8616438

Distributed in the United States by
Houghton Mifflin Company
2 Park Street
Boston, Massachusetts 02108
ISBN: 0-395-66909-X

Distributed in Canada by
Thomas Allen & Son
390 Steelcase Road East
Markham, Ontario L3R 1G2
ISBN: 0-395-66909-X

Distributed in the United Kingdom & Ireland by
GeoCenter International UK Ltd
The Viables Center, Harrow Way
Basingstoke, Hampshire RG22 4BJ
ISBN: 9-62421-510-3

Worldwide distribution enquiries:
Höfer Communications Pte Ltd
38 Joo Koon Road
Singapore 2262
ISBN: 9-62421-510-3

Bienvenue!

Welcome! My first tour of Brittany was by bicycle, a spontaneous, free-wheeling trip where the hills always seemed to go down but rarely up. The memories lingering from that holiday must be similar to those of many first-time visitors—Dinard's classy beach with its rows of elegant striped beach tents, the wayside calvaries with their tearful but forgiving Christs, and the Bretons themselves —women with buckets scabbling in the mud, an old man cycling in his clogs...

Memory tends to gild the past, but on each of my subsequent visits to Brittany I found my first impressions held true. As one 1950's guidebook to the region puts it 'the farthest westward one advances the deeper one seems to plunge into the past.'

My aim in *Insight Pocket Guide: Brittany* is to take visitors to those parts of Brittany that are essentially Breton rather than simply Gallic, in particular to west Brittany, Basse Bretagne. A choice of day-drives and city walks allows you to set your own itinerary, providing the nucleus for a weekend break or—travelling anti-clockwise from St Malo or Roscoff—a pleasant week or fortnight's touring.

The guide opens with five itineraries that take you on day-drives to the popular resorts and secluded beaches of the Emerald and Pink Granite Coasts, over the heathlands of the Armorica Regional Park, through the woods and orchards of Cornouaille, and to the medieval forests inland. Eight options then introduce Brittany's historic cities and ports, guiding you round St Malo and Dinan, Quimper and Vannes. A further four options lead to the best of Brittany's beaches and islands. The sections on history and culture, festivals, shopping and the Breton cuisine are designed to flesh out the background to what you see and experience; a practical information section provides essential tips. Even if your stay here is only a short one, I hope that your memories will be as long and as vivid as mine.

Welcome! Bienvenue! — Nigel Tisdall

Contents

Preceding pages: Mont St Michel, near St Malo.

What to Know

*Following
pages:
typically
Breton.*

Land of King Arthur

Two elements etch the soul of Brittany. First there is the sea, which assaults and tatters the region on three sides, a jagged coastline of rocky protrusions and sandy seclusions that extends for some 750 miles (1,207km). Then there is the granite, the hard grey rocks that form its ancient core, the Armorican Massif. Today the Arrée and Noire moorlands, still described as *montagnes,* remind us of the great mountain chain that once arose here, now weathered low and drowned by a rising sea that has deeply indented the shoreline.

Modern Brittany covers an area of 10,495 square miles (27,184 square km), slightly larger than Wales, and it has as much in common with that country and the others of western Europe's Celtic fringe as it does with the main bulk of France. Indeed it was the Celts arriving here in the 6th century BC who gave the region its first known name—Ar-mor, land of the sea. In due course the inland areas, then covered in dense primeval forests, were christened Argoat, land of the wood. For centuries Brittany would remain a land deeply divided between those who farmed and those who fished, a cultural binary that is only now breaking down as we witness the emergence of a third group—those who cater for the demands of tourists.

The first Celts who settled here must have been as perplexed as we are by the enigmatic megalithic litter that has lain strewn throughout Brittany since 5,000BC. These menhirs, dolmens and cromlechs (the very words we use to describe these monuments and graves are Breton) were the work of neolithic and Early Bronze Age tribes about which we know virtually nothing—save that they left us one of the most elaborate conundrums in prehistory.

Such monuments are only one of the many mysteries that cloud early Breton history and enrich its folklore. Brittany is rightly called a land of legends, a traditional home of King Arthur and his knights, the tempestuous background for the romance of Tristan and Iseult, a fitting location for the drowned city of Ys.

The Christian missionary

Bataille de Brigands, by
Sébastien Vrancx

Culture

A street in Morlaix, 1830, **by Jules Noël**

saints who came here from Britain in the sixth century AD commandeered these myths, just as their disciples capped the pagan megaliths with crosses to proclaim the new religion. Even today the Breton heavens are well-populated with local saints, many of whom have yet to enter the official panoply but who are nevertheless honoured at roadside calvaries, in stained glass, and at the Bretons' unique act of religious devotion, the *pardon*.

This rich spiritual heritage, combined with the region's natural isolation, forged a sense of Breton nationhood that has continually sought to distance itself from the rest of France. In 845 Nominoë, Brittany's first national hero, made this plain when he overthrew the region's Frankish rulers and declared himself head of an independent kingdom.

It was to take another seven hundred years before the French monarchy finally incorporated Brittany into their disparate union of provinces. During these centuries the region became a battleground, firstly for the long-running medieval wars between the French and the English, and secondly for the feuding of its own rival nobles. Yet these times also knew peace, and by the turn of the 15th century the Duchy of Brittany was enjoying its so-called 'golden age' under Duke Jean V—a time of prosperity born of maritime trading and the production of sailcloth.

In 1488 the Duchess Anne succeeded to the Breton throne (see panel) and her marriage to the French King Charles VIII three years later effectively marked the end of Brittany's independence. The region now became a neglected and backward part of France that frequently baulked against the caprices and injustices inflicted by a

Stained glass, Dinan

The Duchess Anne

Crowned Duchess of Brittany at the age of 11, Anne (1477–1514) was the last sovereign to rule over an independent Brittany. When Anne was only 13 it was decided by marital engineers at the French court that she should marry King Charles VIII, then aged 21. It was a tempestuous courtship: Charles besieged Rennes for three months in pursuit of his claim and Anne was forced to seek the annulment of her marriage by proxy to Maximilian of Austria, heir to the Holy Roman Emperor.

They married in 1491 and this union born of politics is said to have kindled a warm love. Seven years later Charles died from an accidental blow to the head and Anne became Queen of France for a second time when she married his rapidly divorced successor, Louis XII, in 1499.

For the next fifteen years Anne was left to govern her Duchy, a swansong reign during which she secured valuable rights of independence for her subjects. When she died in 1514 at the age 37 she was universally mourned, a champion of the Breton cause whose name is now emblazoned on hotels, *créperies* and ferry boats throughout the entire region.

quasi-colonialist central government. Riots, such as the 'Stamped Paper Revolt' of 1675 staged by armed peasants known as the Bonnets Rouges, would be provoked by new taxes on tobacco, grain or salt and always led to vicious reprisals.

Such struggles between an increasingly vociferous peasant class and an outlandish aristocracy were signs of a larger nationwide discontent that eventually boiled over in the French Revolution of 1789. At first the Bretons welcomed these events with their promise of an end to tyranny and new opportunities for self-determination. Within a year though this euphoria had turned to dismay: suddenly the Republicans had reduced Brittany to five meaningless *départements* on a map and were demanding the abolition of the Breton language. Conscription, religious persecution and the execution of the King all brought protesters on to the streets in their thousands. The arrival of the Terror in 1793 provoked open support for the Royalist counter-revolutionaries known as the Chouans (see panel), whose sporadic rebellions lasted until the 1830s.

Napoleon inevitably left his mark on Brittany, most clearly in the grid of streets he built in Pontivy, which for a brief period was known as Napoléonville. Under his instigation straight roads were built through the province and the port of Lorient developed as a naval base. He also ordered the construction of the Nantes-Brest Canal, a response to the disruption of

The Chouans

In Brittany the euphoria inspired by the French Revolution of 1789 soon turned to disillusionment as the Bretons found their hopes for self-determination were not to be realised. By 1793 a resistance movement, the *Association Bretonne,* had been formed with the aim of recovering these former rights. When the reign of terror reverberating around France reached Brittany the atrocities committed in its hunt for counter-revolutionaries only served to win new support for their cause. One of the most barbaric of such incidents occurred in Nantes in October 1793 when the Convention's Deputy, Jean-Baptiste Carrier, chose to clear his overstocked jails by loading prisoners into barges which were then towed out into the Loire and sunk.

Better known by their nickname of the *Chouans* (after the cry of the screech-owl used as an identifying signal), the members of the Association were led by a 22-year-old farmer's son, Georges Cadoudal.

His forces soon became linked with the wider Royalist cause and in 1795 an attempt was made by foreign exiles to land an invasion force on the Quiberon peninsula with support from the British navy. It ended in disaster when the combined Royalist and Chouan armies, whose numbers were considerably less than the 100,000 troops envisaged, marched into a trap laid by the Revolutionary General Louis-Lazare Hoche.

The debâcle ended with some 900 prisoners being taken. Few were pardoned and the defeat marked the virtual end of the Chouans, though not of their cause or Cadoudal. In 1799 he organised new guerrilla forces to fight for Breton liberty but these were soon flushed out. Cadoudal escaped to England, returning in 1804 to launch a bizarre attempt to kidnap Napoleon. Romantically known as 'the last Chouan' he was captured and executed the same year, his body unceremoniously given to anatomy students for dismemberment.

French troops in Tréguier, 1870

Quimper, Brittany's most Celtic city

coastal communication between these ports caused by the English navy. The late 19th century also saw the gradual advance of the railway into Brittany, a *cheval noir* that the peasants would walk miles to see.

When Gauguin arrived in Pont-Aven in 1886 much of Brittany was still devout, conservative, parochial and superstitious. Outwardly it conformed to our severe and idyllic image of Brittany as a hardy land of box-beds and wooden *sabots* (clogs), of threshing-songs and widows waiting on the cliffs for the return of the fishing boats. *Pardons* were still well-attended, the men dressed in their embroidered waistcoats, the women in their elaborate lace head-dresses known as *coiffés*. But it was also a time of insidious social change, principally in the larger cities and ports to which the rural young would drift, many often choosing to better their lot by emigration. Breton culture was also being suppressed, with humiliating measures taken to stamp out its language, such as forcing schoolchildren who spoke Breton to wear a heavy *sabot* around their necks.

These changing horizons were shattered by two world wars. It is said that in the Great War Brittany suffered more deaths per capita than any other part of France. In the Second World War the German Occupation provoked a militant nationalist resistance movement that came to the fore in the weeks preceding D-Day.

The post-war period opened with many of Brittany's cities and ports bombed to the ground. Migrants flooded to other parts of France or abroad, and those that eventually returned came back with new perceptions. Soon traditional Breton clothes and furniture were being rejected in favour of their cheaper and more modern equivalents. In due course the Bretons would sell their elaborately decorated box-beds and bench-chests to the region's early tourists, the 'Kodakers' from Paris who enjoyed that previously unheard of luxury, the paid holiday.

The 1960s saw the start of an economic renaissance in Brittany which continues apace today. The principal catalyst was a young Breton farmer, Alexis Gourvennec, who led a series of protests now known as 'The Artichoke War'. These demonstrations, yet another Breton rebellion against negligent overseers, brought an end to the archaic marketing system that had controlled the sale of agricultural produce in Brittany for centuries. Farmers' co-operatives were established throughout the region which became the focus of a unified clamour for change. One demand was for a deep-water port at Roscoff so that Breton produce could be exported to English markets, a move that led to the creation of Brittany Ferries in 1973 and which has in turn transformed the nature of tourism in the region.

Today Brittany is one of the most prosperous, hi-tech regions of France, and produces more milk, eggs, chickens, beef and field vegetables than any other part of the country. It is still dogged by central controls, though, and the removal of the Loire-Atlantique *département* from the region in 1972, which included its former capital Nantes (and the Muscadet vineyards!), still wrankles.

However economic progress, including the rapid rise in seasonal tourism, has also inspired a new cultural confidence. Today there is a new respect for the Breton language and a surging Celtic pride that actively fosters Brittany's ancient links with its Celtic brethren. For Brittany no longer sees itself as a part of France but—with a forethought typical of a region that has always sought to keep its destiny in its own hands—as a part of Europe.

The Breton Language

The roots of the Breton language are Celtic and visitors familiar with Welsh, Gaelic or Cornish will immediately notice the similarity. Place-names will probably provide your first encounter with its vocabulary—these are often a combination of natural elements—stone (*men*), sea (*mor*), mountain (*menz*) or wind (*avel*)—and function, for example as a port (*pors*), village (*ker*), parish (*plou*) or holy place (*loc*). Thus Huelgoat means 'high wood', and Plouhinec 'place of gorse', while other settlements will be named after local saints such as Guimilau (town of St Miliau).

Today there are many Bretons who can still speak their native tongue, nearly all living along the region's western shores, and Breton is taught in some schools and in the universities of Brest and Rennes, but it's clear that few young people are learning it. It seems likely that Breton, like many other Celtic languages, will become the toy of academics, nationalists and esoteric writers. Peace and prosperity have brought the region a cosmopolitan outlook, giving the lie to the revivalists' slogan '*Hep Brezoneg, Breiz ebed*' ('Without Breton, Brittany doesn't exist.')

BC

450,000: Artefacts found at St Columban, the oldest prehistoric site in Brittany, reveal the presence of nomadic tribes in the region during palaeolithic times.

5,000: Start of the megalith-building period. During the next 3,000 years thousands of stone monuments are erected throughout Brittany by unknown neolithic and Early Bronze Age settlers.

6th century: Celts from Central Europe spread north through Gaul. They give the region its first known name: Armor, land of the sea.

AD

56: Caesar's armies defeat the most powerful tribe in Armorica, the Veneti. The Romans build towns and roads that form the basis of many present-day settlements such as Nantes, Rennes and Vannes.

5th century: The Romans withdraw their legions. As the Anglo-Saxons invade England many native Celts flee across the Channel. Some establish new colonies in Armorica which they rename Little Britain —hence the region's modern name.

6th century: Birth of Breton culture. Celtic mysticism is tempered by the teachings of Christian missionary saints like Malo, Brioc and Pol-de-Léon.

799: Charlemagne, King of the Franks, conquers Brittany. The region becomes part of an empire covering most of western Europe.

826: Charlemagne's son, Louis the Pious, creates the duchy of Brittany. Its first Duke, Nominoë, rebels against Frankish rule to win independence in 845. It is shortlived but marks the establishment of the region's boundaries and the start of Brittany's struggle for self-determination.

919: The Normans overrun Brittany but are expelled twenty years later by the last Breton king, Alain Barbe-Torte. On his death in 952 feuding breaks out between rival nobles.

1066: The Norman Conquest of Britain: from now on the history of Brittany will be forever entangled with the tortured affairs of England and France.

1337: Start of the Hundred Years War between England and France. In Brittany both sides contest the 'War of Succession'.

1341–64: Bertrand du Guesclin rises to fame as a military commander.

1351: 'Battle of the Thirty' takes place near Ploërmel.

1364: The Dukes of Montfort restore order to the region, skilfully pursuing a course of neutrality between rival factions. A century of renewed prosperity and cultural energy ensues as maritime trade flourishes. Many churches built.

1491: Anne of Brittany marries Charles VIII, King of France. Brittany remains an independent duchy but is now effectively a part of France.

1532: The permanent union of Brittany and France is ratified by the Vannes parliament.

1534: Jacques Cartier, born in Rothéneuf, discovers the mouth of the St Lawrence river.

16th–17th centuries: Sporadic periods of lawlessness and rebellion result from the half-hearted efforts of the French monarchy to govern

Brittany. The most serious of these is the revolt of the Bonnets Rouges (1675), a widespread protest by peasants against punitive taxes which is ruthlessly suppressed by the army. As a result the Breton parliament is suspended for 15 years. Construction of parish closes in Finistère.

1722: A drunken carpenter accidentally starts a fire that destroys most of the Breton capital, Rennes.

1789: The French Revolution is welcomed by the Bretons. However the advent of conscription, religious persecution and the Terror, along with the unpopular execution of the King and the banning of the Breton language, brings disillusionment.

1795: The Royalist Chouans become the focus of an attempt to launch a counter-revolution with the help of exiled and foreign forces. A landing on the Quiberon peninsula ends in disaster when the invaders find themselves trapped.

1836: Opening of the Nantes-Brest canal.

1886–95: Gauguin and other artists of the 'Pont-Aven' school working in Cornouaille.

1911: The first Breton separatist party, Strollad Broadel Breisz, is founded.

1914–18: The First World War exacts a heavy death toll.

1939–45: The Second World War. The entire male population of the Ile de Sein are among the first to answer General de Gaulle's call to join him in exile in England. The Breton Resistance smuggles hundreds of Allied airmen across the Channel. Patton's Third Army liberates the region but not before many Breton cities such as St Malo, Brest, Lorient and Nantes are badly damaged.

1960: The 'Artichoke War' becomes the focus for a restructuring of the way Brittany's agricultural produce is marketed. It marks the start of an economic renaissance in the region.

1972: A change of official boundaries removes the Loire-Atlantique *département* from Brittany.

1989: High speed TGV rail link opens between Paris and Brest. One million British and Irish tourists now visit Brittany every year.

Our guide opens with five touring itineraries that will introduce you to the best of Brittany, from its dramatic coasts to the gently wooded interior. Eight optional tours then lead you to the region's historic cities and ports, and four further tours guide you to the best of Brittany's beaches and islands.

Côte d'Emeraude: St Malo to Le Val-André

Brittany's northern shoreline is a rollercoaster of rocky headlands and wide sandy beaches that grow increasingly dramatic the further you venture west. The Emerald Coast, which stretches from the Pointe du Grouin near Cancale (see Option 2 in the Pick and Choose section) west to Le Val-André, offers a picturesque introduction to such charms, a gentle succession of traditional resorts and quiet coves that have provided the setting for many a classic seaside holiday.

This itinerary begins in St Malo and idles westwards along the coast: if you prefer a more demanding day you can easily extend your route to include a morning walk round the medieval town centre of <u>Dinan</u> (see *Pick and Choose* Option 3).

Leave St Malo via St Servan (D168) and cross the **Barrage de la**

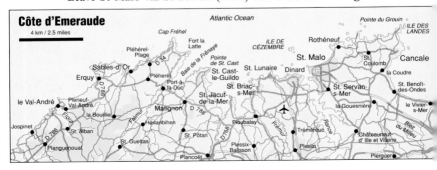

Rance towards Dinard. The road runs along the top of this great dam, built in 1966 and the first in the world to use tidal power to generate elecricity (open daily for half hour visits 8am–8.30pm, tel: 99 46 14 46). To your right you will see the triple towers of the **Tour Solidor**, built in 1382 as part of the Dukes of Montfort's efforts to oversee the unruly Malouins; now a fascinating museum to seafaring around Cape Horn, its present shape dates from 1890 (see *Pick and Choose* Option 1 for opening times).

Soon after you cross the Rance turn right for La Vicomté (D114), a quiet road that leads you into the elegant resort of **Dinard**. Park near the Tourist Office in Boulevard Féart. Deservedly titled 'Queen of the Emerald Coast', Dinard still has aristocratic airs bequeathed to it from the days when Victorian bathing carriages lined its Grand Plage. Blessed with three golden beaches, it was 'discovered' in the 1850s after an American millionaire called Coppinger built a mansion here and inspired a rush of villa-building around St-Énogat. Today Dinard strives to remain stylish, a host to international film festivals and celebrity concerts, its beaches graced by smart rows of striped beach tents and balletic ensembles of straw-hatted *boule* players.

The Emerald Coast

Hôtel La Vallée

For a taste of Dinard's charms walk east from the Tourist Office, down rue de Levavasseur to **Le Grand Hôtel**, built in 1859 with fine views across the Rance to St Malo. It has a relaxing bar, ideal for a late morning coffee or pre-lunch aperitif—try the Hôtel's refreshing George V cocktail, made from champagne, grapefruit juice and *crème de pêche*. From here you can cross the road to the **Yacht Club**, descending some steps to reach the Promenade du Clair de Lune. This walk follows the water's edge round to a small quay where the **Hôtel La Vallée** offers a restful place for an alfresco lunch. Menus here range from the simple to the gourmet—settle for an exquisite bowl of *moules marinière* or get to work on a monster *plateau de fruits de mer*.

From here you can continue to follow the path around the shore to the **Pointe du Moulinet** where a viewing-table maps out the extensive panorama ahead of you. The most noticeable sights are St Malo and the neighbouring island of Grand Bé, and further west the island of Cézembre. The path then curls round the cliffs to the magnificent **Grand Plage**, also known as Plage de l'Écluse, its seafront dominated by the elderly Casino (1911) and the modern Olympic swimming pool (1967). The Tourist Office lies behind these.

Leave Dinard along the D786 towards **St Briac-sur-Mer**, home to one of the oldest golf courses in France. Here the bridge across the Frémur marks the traditional boundary between the *départements* of Ile-et-Vilaine and Côtes d'Armor—in 1990 the latter changed its name from Côtes du Nord after a long campaign to avoid confusion with the eastern *département* Nord. Continue west past the rocket-ship spire of **Lancieux's church**, skirting **Ploubalay** and winding on through **Matignon**. Such villages sport all the characteristic hallmarks of modern Brittany — bullied by traffic, their thick granite walls are bedecked with neon *crêperie* signs and chalked blackboards advertising freshly caught mussels and oysters.

Fort la Latte

Continue along the southern shore of the vast rectangular Baie de la Frênaye, turning right after the bridge at Port-à-la-Duc on to a minor road leading past the Auberge La Licorne. This runs alongside the estuary before climbing inland into woods to join the D16A—follow the signs (a series of right turns) to La Motte and then Fort la Latte.

Built on top of a rocky spur surrounded by crashing waves, **Fort la Latte** is a storybook castle that seems far too picturesque to have seen battle. Set in a park (open daily 10am–12.30pm, 2.30–6.30pm, low season 2.30–5.30pm only), it's a ten minute walk down from the entrance gates to its fortified drawbridges. Constructed in the 13th century by the Goyon-Matignon family, the castle was remodelled in the 17th by the great military architect Vauban.

Dinard's Yacht Club

Its steep walls have played host to a curious parade of historical characters including, in 1715, James Stuart (The Old Pretender) during his ill-fated bid for the English throne, English spies captured after the French Revolution, a troop of White Russians billeted here

Pléhérel-Plage

in the Second World War and, in 1957, the cast of a Hollywood epic starring Kirk Douglas, *The Vikings*. Today only video cameras shoot from its ramparts and the rusty cannon on its outposts lie rotting in the sea-spray, but the Fort still impresses: if you climb up to the watchtower you'll find the commanding views of the north coast are just as they were centuries ago.

Leave Fort la Latte and follow the signs west to **Cap Fréhel** (D16), one of the most panoramic (and popular) headlands in northern Brittany. The tall silhouette of its lighthouse, easily visible from Fort la Latte, dominates the cliffs which rise sheer from the sea to nearly 250ft (75m), the highest part of the Emerald Coast.

After the austere windblown moorland of Cap Fréhel the road (D34A) leads west to a softer landscape of heather and pines where delightful beaches of silvery sand shelter in the cliffs. Here the Breton coast performs one of its enchanting cabarets as every beach you pass appears more magical and inviting than the last. Be sure to stop somewhere for a walk along the shore, perhaps at a small one like **Pléhérel-Plage** where the sunlit water can truly seem emerald-coloured, or at a larger expanse like that at the aptly named resort of **Sables d'Or-les-Pins.**

If you're camping, the sites along this stretch of the coast are idyllic and you should stop soon. Further along the coast (D786) more spectacular beaches greet you—**Erquy** boasts an enormous stretch of pale golden sand, as does **Le Val-André** further west. Both of these resorts have modest hotels ideal for passing travellers who like a long evening stroll on the sands and a quiet night's rest. Strung out along an infinite sea-front, Le Val-André has a particularly beguiling period feel, part-Victorian, part-Thirties. For an enjoyable meal to crown your day the **Hôtel-Restaurant de la Mer** here offers thoughtful home-cooking based on local seafood (63 Rue A Charner. Tel: 96 72 20 44).

Cap Fréhel lighthouse

24

Côte de Granit Rose: Paimpol to St Michel-en-Grève

Stretching unevenly from Paimpol to Trébeurden, the Pink Granite Coast is an undulating landscape of wide beaches and low cliffs fringed with reefs and outlying rocks. Strewn with enormous boulders, many of which have been eroded into curious shapes, it has a surreal aspect most obvious when the evening sun ignites the pink granitic rocks that blush their deepest between Trégastel and Trébeurden.

Granite boulder, Trégastel

While most of this itinerary can be covered in a day it is best spread over two, something essential if you plan to visit the Ile de Bréhat or linger on the beach for any length of time. Tréguier or Port Blanc might be convenient places to break your journey. As in many parts of northern Brittany the coast here is graced by a multitude of quiet coves and splendid beaches that offer a relaxed alternative to the busy resorts, so be sure to have the ingredients for an impromptu picnic on board.

The itinerary begins at the Pointe de Bilfot, from which there is a fine panorama of the Bay of Paimpol. It can be easily reached if you take the D77 east from Plouézec, 6.4 miles (4km) south of Paimpol—go beyond a signpost declaring 'Panorama' to the Pointe itself, where inevitably there is a viewing-table. From here the views extend north-west to the Ile de Bréhat and east to Cap Fréhel, while below an aquamarine sea relentlessly pummels the rocks. In this windswept corner of Brittany the sea has determined life for many Bretons, for from the 1850s up until the turn of the century huge fishing fleets would sail out from Paimpol to catch cod off Iceland,

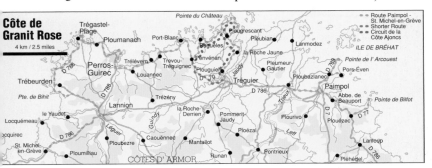

Tréguier cathedral

deep-sea voyages of great hardship and tragedy that were recorded in Pierre Loti's famous novel *Pêcheur d'Islande* (1886).

Return to Plouézec and turn right along the D786 towards Paimpol. Soon you will pass the attractive Gothic ruins of the **Abbey of Beauport**, founded in 1202 (open in summer 9am–noon, 2–7pm). Continue on the D786 through Paimpol to take the D789 signposted north to Ploubazlanec. Turn right here down a minor road to Pors Even.

Pors-Even remains a quiet fishing village, its low granite houses pleasantly devoid of the gaudy trappings of seasonal tourism. Near to the quay the no-nonsense **Café du Port** serves excellent seafood at modest prices. Its terrace, ruled by a *madame* who will visibly wither should you even think of ordering a *crêpe,* is an ideal place to sit and watch the boats bobbing in the bay as you tuck into a plate of *praires* (clams) or *araigneés* (spider crabs).

Return to Ploubazlanec and turn right along the D789 to Pointe de l'Arcouest. This is the embarkation point for the short crossing to the **Ile de Bréhat**, probably your best chance to enjoy some sea air and a walk round one of the mildest of Brittany's many islands (see Option 9 in the *Pick and Choose* section).

From Pointe de l'Arcouest it is simplest to return to Paimpol and and take the D786 to Tréguier. As you head west through a patchwork of cabbage fields you'll notice how the landscape is gaining a more Breton aspect: junctions are adorned with roadside calvaries, street-names are given in French and Breton, Celtic place-names become more common—often prefixed by *ker* (house or village), *plou* (parish) or *lann* (heath). The churches change too, now capped by graceful lantern towers with needle points that pierce the skyline.

Soon the silhouette of Tréguier's cathedral appears on the horizon, the principal city along the Côte de Granit Rose. **Tréguier** sits on a hill overlooking the confluence of the Jaudy and Guindy rivers—after crossing the bridge stay with the river till you reach the place Géneral de Gaulle (look for the Hôtel L'Estuaire), where you turn left and climb up to the place du Martray. This square is the heart of the city, dominated by the splendid **Cathedral of St Tugdual**. Opposite its entrance, in a typically French juxtaposition, a parade of *pâtisseries* and *salons de thé* enable visitors to combine spiritual edification with bodily fortification.

The cathedral is a masterly example of how Breton architects and stonemasons contrived to make a hard and difficult stone like granite sing. It has three towers—the Romanesque 'Hastings' tower, an incomplete Gothic tower above the transept and an 18th-century spire, decoratively aerated with holes to prevent the wind destroying it.

Although dedicated to one of Brittany's 'founder-saints' St Tugdual, a Welsh monk who

Tomb of St. Yves, Tréguier Cathedral

founded a bishopric here in the 6th-century, the cathedral is more obviously a shrine to a more recent, locally-born saint, **St Yves**. As soon as you enter the porch look right and you will see a carved wooden image of him, traditionally depicted standing between a rich and poor man.

Born in 1253 St Yves practised as a lawyer and has become the legal profession's patron saint—across the aisle his tomb, destroyed in the lawless days of the French Revolution, is a 19th-century copy

Memorial to a Breton sailor

of a monument erected in his honour by Duke Jean V, who chose to be buried alongside him.

If you like pottering along minor roads take the D8 north from Tréguier to Plougiel and turn right down the paltry V3, signposted to La Roche Jaune. This marks the start of the 'Circuit de la Côte Ajoncs', an hour-long scenic route that weaves in and around the coast—expect to see a lot of cabbages and artichokes and don't be surprised if the road signs suddenly dry up. They soon re-appear and will lead you out via Plougrescant to the **Pointe du Château** where the departing tide leaves vast swathes of glistening mud and seaweed-fringed rocks. Along here fig trees testify to the mild climate of this Ajoncs (gorse) shore and the boulders have a genuinely pinky hue worthy of a Côte de Granit Rose.

The 'Circuit' eventually leads you through Buguéles to **Port Blanc,** which can be reached more directly from Tréguier by the D70/74. Once a neon-free example of 'undiscovered' Brittany, Port Blanc still has an away-from-it-all charm with its photogenic chapel sited on a rock regularly cut off by the tide. Here the **Hôtel des Iles and** the **Hôtel Le Grande** have restaurants serving good Breton food. Alternatively further west along the D113 there is a temptingly large pale sand beach at Trévou-Tréguignec.

From here you can take the D38 to Trélévern where a minor road (sign-posted to Perros-Guirec) leads you to Louannec. Take the D6 that drops down through chestnut woods to Perros-Guirec, where you should keep to the shore-side road (boulevard de la Mer) which skirts the port and climbs up to a good viewpoint overlooking the **Plage de Trestrignel**. You are now back in the candy-floss world of the seaside holiday — Perros-Guirec is one of the most popular resorts along this stretch of coast and its liveliest beach is the Plage de Trestraou. Your best escape route is the D788 which is known as the Bretonne Corniche, a grand title for what

is a rather average coastal road linking the resorts of Trégastel-Plage and Trébeurden.

Breton fishing boat

The main attractions here are the seaside and the famous pink granite rocks. For pink granite you need look no further than the buildings around you, many of which are faced with this glistening stone, as is the bridge you cross at Ploumanach. For the more dramatic rocks that time has eroded into anthropomorphic shapes turn right by the church in Trégastel and head down to the **Plage du Coz-Porz**. There are more further round the promontory at **Grève Blanche**.

Just past Trébeurden the Pointe de Bihit (turn right off the D788) offers the chance of a view back along this coast and west towards Roscoff. From here a minor coastal road leads you back up to the D65—continue on through Lannion and out on the D786, signposted to Morlaix. Your destination is **St Michel-en-Grève**, one of the most magnificent beaches in Brittany. Its bay cradles a 3 mile (5km) runway of pale white sand, packed so hard it is sometimes used as a horse track for the Lannion races. If the tide's out it's an exhilarating walk of over a mile (1.6km) to find the sea.

Port Blanc

Day 3

Parc Régional d'Armorique: Huelgoat to Locronan

This itinerary takes you through the best of the Parc Régional d'Armorique, a gentle descent from the woods and moorlands of the Monts d'Arrée to the windswept cliffs of the Presqu'île de Crozon. It's a long drive but an easy one and an early start will make it even more pleasurable—be sure to get to Camaret by 1pm if you want lunch!

The route begins in **Huelgoat**, a popular inland centre for walking and hiking in the surrounding hills and forests (see *Pick and Choose* Option 12). Dotted around the Parc there are also 15 well-thought-out specialist museums that provide an engaging introduction to life in Finistère past and present (see 'Museums' in the *Activities* section).

Leave Huelgoat on the D14 in the direction of Loqueffret. The

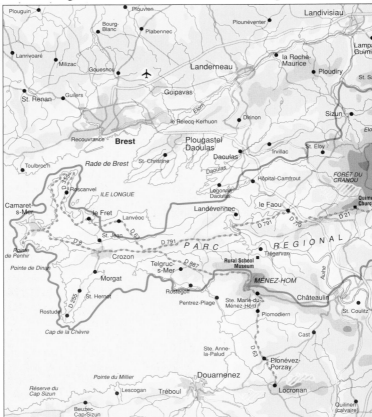

Chapel of St Herbot

road skirts the southern edge of the **Monts d'Arrée**, a ridge of flat granite moorland that can only just be called mountains today—their most accessible high point is the nearby **Roc Trévezel** (1260ft/384m) from which there are sweeping views of the surrounding countryside. Four miles (7km) from Huelgoat you'll find the square-towered **Chapel of St Herbot**, a lovingly tended village church with a small lichen-blotched calvary. St Herbot is the patron saint of horned cattle and at the annual *pardon* held every May farmers would bring their cattle here and solemnly conduct them round the chapel. In time this became impractical so today tufts of hair from their tails are left as an offering on the two stone tables at the base of the chancel.

Continue on through Loqueffret to Croas-Ahars where you turn right for **Brasparts** (D21). The village has a 16th-century parish close and calvary. As you carry on look out for your right for the skeletal ruin of **Quimerch church**, abandoned in the 1870s because it was thought to be too far from the centre of its parish. Further on you pass through the village of Ty-Jopic where you take the D770 to Le Faou.

From Le Faou take the D791 corniche road west for the Crozon Peninsula.

Pointe de Penhir

Soon the sea appears to your right and at Pont de Térénez you cross the Aulne estuary. Now you are on the cross-shaped **Crozon Peninsula**, renowned for its wild and windy coastline but still blessed by a climate mild enough to line the road with farms selling honey, pears and cider. The road rides the spine of this *presqu'île* with views either way to the sea.

At Tal-ar-Groas turn right (D63) for Lanvéoc and then turn left here (D55) for Le Fret. Continue on past the nuclear submarine base at Ile Longue to Roscanavel (D355) and the **Pointe des Espagnols**. From this bleak point there are good views across the bay to Brest: the Pointe gets its name from an incident in 1594 during the Breton Wars of Religion when 400 Spaniards occupied the headland—they were only dislodged after a six week struggle by 4,000 French and English troops. All along this coast you will find the ruins of forts built to defend the peninsula, many of which were the work of Vauban.

Continue round the coast on the D355 to **Camaret**, a quiet fishing port with some excellent quayside fish restaurants. One of the best is on the first floor of the **Hôtel de France** (Quai G Toudouze, tel: 98 27 93 06). This is the place to splash out on a platter of *fruits de mer* or don a bib in readiness for some *homard à la Armoricaine*. The restaurant overlooks the port with its red brick fort built by Vauban in the 1690s and now a naval museum (open daily June–September). The harbour was the site where in 1801 the American inventor Robert Fulton conducted trials of one of the world's earliest submarines.

The best place to walk off your lunch is the bracing air of the **Pointe de Penhir**, a short distance westwards on the D8. This is a bizarre cliff-top land's end, often packed with visitors who appear to have assembled in the hope of some divine visitation but who eventually make do with a contemplative stare at some sea-buffeted rocks known as the **Tas de Pois** (Pile of Peas). An imposing breeze-block monument to the Breton Resistance dominates one rocky spur.

From here you can take the D8 back to Crozon, continuing east in the direction of Châteaulin (D887). As you rejoin the mainland the landscape returns to wild moorland. Look for a turn off to your left for the **Ménez-Hom**, one of Brittany's highest points (1082ft/330m). The peak is essential viewing.

Return to the D887 where you will soon pass the pretty **Chapel**

Pointe de Penhir,
Resistance Monument

of St Mary of the Ménez-Hom. Turn right here onto the D47, sign-posted to Quimper and continue through Plomodiern and Plonévez-Porzay to the postcard-perfect town of Locronan.

Locronan's Renaissance houses were built when Locronan was the centre of a canvas-making industry that supplied sailcloth to the French and Spanish navies. In the late 17th-century Louis XIV abolished the Breton monopoly on linen and Locronan's fortunes soon declined. Today the harmonious ensemble of granite buildings around its central cobbled square are in that state of aesthetic decay which makes many visitors go weak at the knees, including film directors—Roman Polanski turned the square into a pseudo-Wessex village for his film *Tess*.

Around 7pm there is a magical hour when the town falls quiet—this is the time (early in the morning is another) to wander its mossy streets. Be sure to venture down rue Moal where there is the delightful Chapel of Our Lady of Good News, its simple stonework reflected in a large 17th-century rectangular fountain. If you plan to stay here consider sleeping in the Hôtel du Prieuré (Tel: 98 91 70 89), an adequate two star Logis, and eating in the Fer à Cheval restaurant (place d'Église, Tel: 98 91 70 74).

Locronan, Chapel of Our Lady of Good News

DAY 4

Cornouaille: Bénodet to Mur-de-Bretagne

The south-west coast of Brittany is known as Cornouaille, named by the Celts who fled here from Cornwall in the 6th century BC. Here Brittany takes on a softer aspect, a benign landscape of gentle hills and wooded estuaries where high-hedged lanes and cider orchards remind one of England's West Country.

The itinerary meanders along this verdant shore, passing through

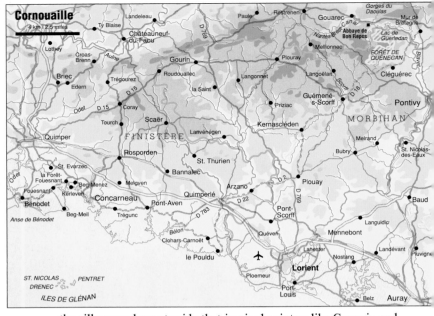

the villages and countryside that inspired painters like Gauguin and Corot, then heading inland to the dark forests of the Argoat. It is best taken over two days, particularly if you plan to go walking—the oak woods around Pont-Aven or the larger Forêt de Quénécan is ideal for this. Quimperlé or Le Pouldu are quiet and convenient places to break your journey. Another alternative is to carry straight on from Le Pouldu to the megaliths and beaches of Carnac (see *Pick and Choose* Option 7).

The itinerary begins in **Bénodet**, a classic sand 'n' mud resort where every summer the roads turn to a thick jam of GB number-plates. Its position at the mouth of the Odet estuary is a winning formula where holidaymakers can happily combine messing about on the river with seaside indolence. If you're arriving from Quimper (D34) take the avenue de l'Odet from the town centre and look for a pull-off (avenue de Kercréven) with a good view of the Odet and Bénodet's **Porte de Plaisance**. The port was one of 37 in France to be awarded an EC Blue Flag for cleanliness in the early '90s.

From here you can continue round along the Corniche de l'Estuaire and the Corniche de la Mer as Bénodet's long stretch of sheltered beach unrolls beside you. The road leads out to the **Pointe de Bénodet** where there are views of the coast and yet more sandy beaches to the east. Here you will also see your first trees felled by the 'hurricane' of 15 October 1987, winds that wrecked many of Brittany's forests and left a trail of devastation that will be an inescapable companion on your journey.

From here the road (Route du Poulinc) curls inland to join the D44, where you turn right for Fouesnant. Continue on to La Forêt-Fouesnant, where you turn right down a minor road as soon as you've crossed the bridge—signposted 'Concarneau par la côte'. This

Concarneau ramparts

route takes you down some delightful lanes lined with chestnut woods and cider orchards, past the fine beach of Kerleven to Beg-Menez, where you turn right (v1 to Concarneau) down a steep hill.

Concarneau is one of the biggest fishing ports in France out of which fleets sail as far as West Africa to catch tunny fish. Its principal attraction is the well-preserved 14th-century **Ville Close** built on an island in the centre of the harbour. As you enter the port keep to the water's edge—you will pass a small chapel on the Quai de la Croix before arriving at the Quai Pénéroff. Here you can park and walk across the small bridge leading to the old town. Inside you will find a quaint tourist-trap grinning with flower-bedecked souvenir shops and restaurants. It is a place to amble through, perhaps pausing for a *crêpe* or *plat du jour*. There is a short rampart walk you can do starting just beside the entrance and a little further on is the comprehensive **Musée de la Peche** with rooms devoted to the extraction of whales, tuna, herring and sardines from the sea (open daily 9.30am–7pm 15 June–15 September; rest of the year 9.30am–12.30pm, 2–6pm).

Leave Concarneau on the D783, signposted to Quimperlé. The road weaves through Trégunc to **Pont-Aven**: when you arrive don't cross the bridge but continue straight on to park by the port. From here you can walk across a small footbridge, past one of Pont-Aven's

Concarneau harbour

Gauguin and the School of Pont-Aven

The tourist brochures would have you believe that Paul Gauguin (1848–1903) and his fellow bohemians came to Pont-Aven for the beautiful landscape and excellent *crêpes*. In fact, they came here because they were poor and Brittany was cheap. By the time Gauguin arrived in 1886 there was already an established artists' colony in Pont-Aven, part of a regular summer exodus from the Paris studios. Gauguin soon fell out of step with these Salon painters whose slick, photograph-like depictions of Breton life he detested. His objectives were more emotional: 'I love Brittany' he declared, 'I find there the savage, the primitive. When my clogs resound on this granite soil I hear the dull, matt, powerful tone that I'm after in my painting.'

The arrival of Émile Bernard in Pont-Aven in 1888 proved catalytic. Bernard re-awakened Gauguin to the piety and religious devotion of the Breton people which became a common subject for their work. They painted in a deliberately crude, almost caricatural manner using brilliant colours and fluid dark outlines around their subjects that became known as Synthesism—Gauguin's *La Vision après le Sermon. La Lutte de Jacob avec l'Ange* is one of the best known examples, inspired by the local *pardon* at Pont-Aven.

The following year Gauguin left the crowds of Pont-Aven for the peace of Le Pouldu, another step in a life-long process of rejection that would eventually lead him to the South Seas. At Le Pouldu, Synthesist ideas were advanced further by artists like Sérusier, Laval, de Haan and Filiger. Their work was always primarily an exploration of abstract problems—how line, colour and rhythm could be used to express mood, emotion and imagination—with the Breton landscape and its people providing a launchpad for their investigations. Today Gauguin is credited as a major figure in the liberation of art from obedience to nature, but the work of the Pont-Aven school should be

Bretonne de Profil (1892), by
Cuno Aimet

seen as more than an adjunct to his achievement. It provides a striking record of a Brittany that has all but vanished, a severe and superstitious land of starched *coiffés* and *pardons* where life was guided by the seasons and occasionally brightened by dancing, wrestling and regattas.

many old water-mills, and back along the rue Auguste Brizeux to the town centre.

First impressions of Pont-Aven are unfavourable, for this once-quiet village where Gauguin and other artists came to paint in the 1880s is now an artless and commercial shrine to their achievements. Today the town has some 40 art galleries bathing in the master's after-glow—ignore them all and head straight for the **Musée de Pont-Aven** in the place de l'Hôtel de Ville (open 10am–12.30pm, 2–7pm daily, closed 4 January–22 March). The museum has no original Gauguins (just look at the biscuit tins on sale everywhere to see what he was painting) but it does provide a quick introduction to the works and aspirations of the Pont-Aven school (see panel).

From the Musée it's a short walk down to the Tourist Office where you should ask for their free guide to the forest walks and painting-spotting trails around Aven. Be sure to make the hour-long walk up through the Bois d'Amour to the exquisite **Tremalo chapel** which still houses the gaunt yellow figure of Christ that featured in Gauguin's famous *Le Christe Jaune* of 1889.

Leave Pont-Aven by the D783, signposted to Quimperlé. At Riec-sur-Bélon turn right onto the D24 which weaves around the Bélon estuary, home of the famous Bélon oyster, to Clohars-Carnoët. Shortly after here turn right for Le Pouldu *plage* (D124).

Le Pouldu is where Gauguin and company moved to in the winter of 1889 and it has few of the tourists trappings that have overwhelmed Pont-Aven. Apart from its peaceful setting the main reason for a visit here is to see the **Maison Marie Henry**, a diligent reconstruction of the inn where Gauguin, Sérusier, Bernard, Filiger and others stayed (rue des

Top: Tremalo chapel
Right: Goose by Gauguin,
Maison Marie Henry

Le Pouldu

Grandes-Sables, open 1 June–30 September daily, 10am–1pm, 2–7pm, guided visits only). Known as the 'Buvette de la Plage' its actual site was next door (now the Thirties-style Café de la Plage) but the museum maintains an authentic air: in the dining room, where the walls were playfully decorated by the artists, there are two original works—a wistful angel by Filiger and a robust white goose by Gauguin.

Leave Le Pouldu heading north for Quimperlé (D49), a delightful ride through the mellow Forêt de Carnoët. At Quimperlé you cross the River Laïta and take the D22 to Plouay, a quiet country road that bursts into colour when the leaves turn in autumn. Pass through Plouay, turning left as you leave the town onto the minor D178, signposted to Kernascléden, which runs along the edge of the Forêt de Pont-Calleck.

Brittany is a land that can seem tiresomely over-stocked with churches, but the one at Kernascléden is certainly worth seeing. A fine example of an inconsequential village cradling a bloated religious edifice at its centre, Kernascléden's church was built in 1453 by the Rohan family. Its grey-green granite, tamed by masons and adulterated by weather, may well be text-book Brittany but the slim tower, rose windows and stone-vaulted interior testify to the efforts of the builders to make this one something special.

Inside to your right you'll find the scene painters' contribution, faded frescoes depicting the Dance of Death and a Hell where sinners are flayed, boiled and blinded as a preliminary to being chewed by grinning devils, mangled in barrels and skewered by trees.

Gauguin's haunt, Café de la Plage

38

Suitably cautioned, continue along the D782 to Guémené-sur-Scorff and take the D18 to **Mur-de-Bretagne** via Cléguérec. Park in the place d'Église, where there is a Pavillon du Tourisme. The *crêperie* **Les Blés d'Or** next door is a spotlessly clean restaurant popular with the locals, ideal for a light meal and a perusal of the day's *Ouest-France*. You'll find Mur-de-Bretagne is an easy-going inland resort, perfect for walking and outdoor activities on and around the Lac de Guerlédan (see *Pick and Choose* Option 12).

Morbihan: Vannes to Paimpont

This itinerary takes you into the quiet forests and valleys of inland Brittany, travelling along back roads to medieval ruins and castles and to the ancient woods of Brocéliande, long known as a setting for Arthurian legends.

It begins in the lively city of **Vannes**, Brittany's medieval capital (see Option 8 in the *Pick and Choose* section). Escaping it is not easy—look for signs to Ploërmel or Redon (not Josselin), for you need to get onto the N166 going east. Five miles (8km) from Vannes you turn left (N166) towards Elven. Shortly after this junction look for a turning left signposted 'Forteresse de Largoët', its entrance marked by two stone pillars. Better known as the **Tours d'Elven**, this former castle is now an impressive ivy-clad ruin that can still

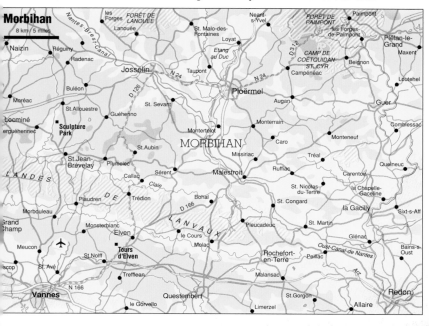

The Tours d'Elven

evoke the thud of history. Drive on to its main entrance gate and park; from here it's a pleasant 25-minute walk through chestnut woods to the castle.

Begun in 1236 the castle was rebuilt in the 15th century by the Marshal de Rieux, one of Duke François II's officers. It was all but razed to the ground in 1488 by Charles VIII as punishment for François' part in an attempt to overthrow him. Today only two of an original eleven towers remain—an overgrown round tower, now partly restored, and the imposing six-storey keep. Rising spectacularly to 144ft (44m) the keep's lower walls are as thick as 29ft (9m) in places—looking up from the interior (beware dive-bombing pigeons) you can still see the huge fireplaces and stairways of this medieval skyscraper.

A genuine damsel-in-distress prison, the Tours d'Elven are said to have played host to a future English king, Henry VII, held captive here in 1476. They were also the setting of a popular 19th-century romantic novel by Octave Feuillet, *Roman d'un Jeune Homme Pauvre* (yes, the hero jumps from the tower to prove his love for the young girl imprisoned in the keep...). Today the towers are the scene of a nocturnal *son-et-lumière* based on Arthurian themes—it's a credit to these stoic ruins that their enchantment remains undiminished by the gubbins the show has scattered everywhere (performances July-August only, details from Tourist Offices).

Return to the N166 and continue into the village of Elven, turning left on its outskirts (D1) for Trédion. This minor road takes you into the **Landes de Lanvaux**, once moorland but now a fertile and wooded upland with scattered settlements. In the 1790s the Chouans set up an independent kingdom here and in

Josselin Castle

the Second World War it was a frequent place of refuge for the Resistance. Keep on the D1 through Trédion to **Callac** where you turn left (v5/6) towards St Aubin. **Callac's church** has a calvary with particularly expressive faces; on the outskirts you will pass an elaborate grotto, a copy of the one at Lourdes. A little further on a small Logis, the **Moulin de Callac**, provides the chance for a drink and a *crêpe* in the peace of the countryside.

Continue to St Aubin, past the church and on north (v6) towards Cruguel, turning left at an unsigned T-junction to join the D126 to **Josselin**. Piled up on the banks of the River Oust this medieval town has long been overwhelmed by the mighty bulk of Josselin castle. As you draw near you'll see its steep walls greeting you with solid defiance—don't be daunted for as you cross the bridge and climb up into the town you'll find it's just a façade—only three towers of its original nine survive today, the rest pulled down by Cardinal Richelieu in 1629.

Try to park at the top of the town near the basilica Notre Dame du Roncier (but not on a Saturday which is market day). From here it's a short walk to the town's half-timbered hub, the place Notre Dame. For a light lunch try the **Café du Centre** in the square; for something more substantial consider the **Auberge de Clisson** (just up from the basilica) or the **Hôtel du Commerce** (9 rue Glatinier) which has a restaurant overlooking the river.

Josselin castle's impressive facade

which has a restaurant overlooking the river.

To visit the castle cut through the slim rue du Château to its main entrance in place de la Congrégation, next to the Tourist Office. All visits are guided with some English commentary provided (open July–August 10am–12pm, 2–6pm; June and September 2–6pm; April–May Wednesdays, Sundays and Public Holidays 2–6pm). The exterior façade is its most impressive feature, a tableau of ornamented granite that frequently incorporates the letter A, a tribute to the much-loved Duchess Anne. The interior, much of it restored in the 19th century, is a pompous amalgam of the portraits, mottos and logos of the Rohan family, the castle's owners since 1407.

Visitors may well prefer to repair to the nearby Musée des Poupées, a doll museum housed in the castle's former stables (open same hours), which reveals the toys and ploys used to keep *les enfants* quiet from the ancient days of miniature silver tea-sets to the plastic *croissants* and TGV trains of today.

Spare some time for the basilica too, its exterior spiked with lewd, jutting gargoyles. Founded in the 11th century it is dedicated to Our Lady of the Bramble Bush who is said to have been discovered under such a bush in the 9th century. On the opposite side of her white stone altar lies the beatific tomb of Oliver and Marguerite de Clisson—one-time owner and re-builder of Josselin castle, he rose

to become Constable of France in 1380; his brutality during the Hundred Years' War earnt him the title—'Butcher of the English'. The worshippers beneath them were beheaded during the French Revolution.

From Josselin the itinerary continues east but lovers of art

Tomb of Oliver and Marguerite de Clisson

ern sculpture park at **Kerguéhennec**. Set in the grounds of a very desirable and aristocratic-looking18th-century château it lies 7½ miles (12km) west of Josselin (take the N24 to St Allouestre then go south on the D11). The sculpture park offers visitors an aesthetic treasure-hunt through avenues of trees mined with witty, moving and downright baffling works by sculptors from all over Europe (open daily April–October, 10am–7pm).

To resume the itinerary leave Josselin on the D129/N24 to Ploërmel. One-and-a-half miles (2km) out of town the road bisects around 'La Pyramide', a monument to commemorate the site of the **Combat des Trente** of 1351. The 'Battle of the Thirty' tried to settle a long-running feud between French and English factions garrisoned in the castles of Josselin and Ploërmel during the War of the Breton Succession. Each side sent 30 knights to contest their cause in what was billed as a tournament (it was officially a time of truce) but which became a famous day of chivalry and carnage recorded in Froissart's *Chronicles*. It ended with eight dead and many wounded—the Bretons were declared the victors but the war rumbled on for another thirteen years.

Combat des Trente monument

Continue on the N24, by-passing Ploërmel (follow the signs to Rennes), till you reach Campénéac. Turn left here onto the D312 for **Paimpont**, a slate-and-granite market town that is the natural centre for exploring the Forêt de Paimpont (see *Pick and Choose* Option 12. If you plan to stay here the **Relais de Brocéliande** (Tel: 99 07 81 07) is warm and friendly and has an enjoyable restaurant.

Kerghuéhennec sculpture park

1. St Malo

St Malo is one of the most appealing of the Channel ports and you should head straight for its granite-walled heart, known as the *cité intra-muros*. The city gets its name from Maclou, a Welsh monk who arrived here in the 6th-century to spread the Christian message. For many centuries it was a well-fortified island, only linked to the mainland by a long causeway, from where the Malouins ruled the Rance and the high seas beyond.

In 1534 Jacques Cartier, born in nearby Rothéneuf, discovered

the St Lawrence River and it was from here that settlers sailed in 1698 to colonise the Iles Malouines, better known to us as Las Malvinas or The Falklands. In the 17th and 18th-centuries St Malo's corsairs regularly plundered the English, Dutch and Spanish fleets, their piracy proving so profitable that its shipowners could afford to build solid country mansions, known as *malouiniéres,* in the neighbouring town of St Servan (see panel on page 48).

St Malo was severely bombed in 1944 and what you see today is an impressive reconstruction of the old city, built mainly in

View from St Malo's ramparts

an 18th-century style. Park outside its walls, either alongside the Port de Plaisance or in the Esplanade St Vincent where the Tourist Office is located. The best way to see St Malo is to take a leisurely walk around its ramparts: they appear stern and foreboding at first but as the tide retreats you'll discover golden beaches nestling at their feet. You get up to the **ramparts** by some steps in the right-

hand side of the Porte St Vincent, but before you ascend them wander a short way up the **rue Garangeau** (straight ahead from the place Chateaubriand) and buy a *pâtisserie* or some chocolate sardines to help you through the expedition.

Make the walk clockwise, first passing by the pleasure boats in the **Bassin Vauban** and over the **Grande Porte**. Turn the corner at the **Bastion St Louis** where there is a bewigged statue of the gallant corsair René Duguay-Trouin (1673–1736). Down on the roundabout another of St Malo's famous sons is honoured: Mahé de la Bourdonnais (1699–1753), who took a leading role in the colonisation of Mauritius. As you near the next bastion, **St Philippe**, your views extend across the mouth of the Rance to Dinard. Here the long Môle des Noires stretches seawards and the power of the waves becomes more apparent: the tidal range around St Malo can be well over 33ft (10m).

The walk turns again to skirt the large **Bastion de la Hollande**: between here and the Tour Bidouane are some of the city's oldest ramparts dating from the Middle Ages, with Plage de Bon Secours below. As you continue round you will see the island of **Grande Bé**, which can be reached on foot at low tide. The writer René de Chateaubriand is buried there, one of Brittany's best known authors.

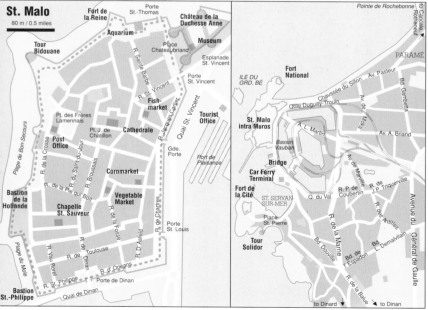

St. Malo

80 m / 0.5 miles

Fort de la Reine
Porte St.-Thomas
Aquarium
Tour Bidouane
Château de la Duchesse Anne
Museum
Place Chateaubriand
Esplanade St. Vincent
Porte St. Vincent
R. Sainte Barbe
R. St. Vincent
Fish-market
Pl. des Frères Lamennais
Pl. J. de Chatillon
Post Office
R. de la Crosse
R. du St-Jour
R. Broussais
R. Jacques Cartier
Quai St. Vincent
Cathedrale
Tourist Office
Gde. Porte
Cornmarket
R. de la Pie qui Boit
Vegetable Market
Bastion de la Hollande
Chapelle St. Sauveur
R. de la Fosse
R. d'Asfeld
R. de Chartres
Porte St. Louis
Plage de Bon Secours
Plage du Môle
R. Vau Borel
R. de Dinan
R. de Toulouse
Bd. d'Orléans
R. St. Philippe
Porte de Dinan
Bastion St.-Philippe
Quai de Dinan

Pointe de Rochebonne
to Cancale, Rothéneuf
PARAMÉ
ILE DU GRD. BÉ
Fort National
Chaussée du Sillon
Av. Pasteur
Bd. Gambetta
Quai Duguay-Trouin
St. Malo intra Muros
A. L. Martin
Av. du Môle
Av. A. Briand
Bassin Vauban
Bridge
Av. de Marville
R. P. de Coubertin
R. de J.-P. Triqueville
Car Ferry Terminal
Fort de la Cité
ST. SERVAN-SUR-MER
Q. du Val
Place St. Pierre
R. des Antilles
Avenue du Général de Gaulle
Tour Solidor
Bd. de la Marne
Bd. Douville
Bd. de l'Espadon
Bd. de L. Demalvilain
R. de la Balue
to Dinard
to Dinan

René de Chateaubriand

Chateaubriand (1768–1848) was born in St Malo too and the bizarre childhood he endured at the family château in Combourg is amusingly chronicled in his *Mémoires d'Outre-Tombe*.

Next to the **Tour Bidouane** there is a small garden with a frantic statue of the corsair Robert Surcouf (1773–1827). Nearby is a cultural centre fostering the age-old links between St Malo and Quebec. Turning the corner again the views are now east to Paramé and out to the Fort National, built in 1689 by Vauban and again only accessible at low tide. The next bastion, **Fort de la Reine**, leads you towards the Porte St Vincent where there are steps down to the place Chateaubriand. To your left are the towers and turrets of **St Malo's Castle**. It houses the city's museum, most interesting for the insight into the maritime adventures of local heroes like Cartier, Surcouf, and Duguay-Trouin (open daily from Easter to October 9am–noon, 2–6pm).

Within the *cité* itself you'll find a cosy, cobbled network of narrow streets lined with expensive shops and more reasonably priced restaurants. It's ideal for wandering and browsing in.

If you're on your way home St Malo's also a perfect port of call

St Malo's Castle

for some last minute shopping before you dash for the ferry. Here you can pick up all those things Breton you meant to buy but never actually did: for *faïence* try **Morly**, No. 6 rue Porcon de la Barbinais, and for folkloric souvenirs and *specialités régionales* the shops in rue Broussais. If you're searching for a little *cadeau* **Le Comptoir**, 5 rue des Merciérs (just off the place de la Poissonnerie) has a useful range of mustards, pâtés, and liqueurs while the **Galerie Guinemer**, 13 rue Jacques Cartier, has an above-average selection of watercolours and lithographs by Breton artists, mainly on maritime themes.

Eating out in St Malo is a far from arduous task. The rue Jacques Cartier offers visitors a pleasant choice of pavement restaurants and

in the side streets off it you'll find plenty of *crêperies*. If you find life *intra-muros* getting a bit claustrophobic take yourself off to the quieter **St Servan** which has a good beach and the solid **Tour Solidor**, home to an unusual museum to the sailors of the Cape Horn (open 9.30am–noon, 2–6.30pm daily low season closed Tuesdays). Some of the exhibits, such as the decorated rolling-pins given by mariners to their loved ones, bear witty ditties that may explain why St Malo's explorers and privateers really put to sea:

"From rocks and sands and barren lands
Kind fortune keep me free,
And from great guns and women's tongues
Good Lord deliver me."

St Malo

Robert Surcouf, statue in St Malo

The Corsairs Of St Malo

In the 17th-century St Malo was the largest port in France, a proud and impregnable island fortress whose privateers were the scourge of the oceans. Born of the long-running feuds between France and Britain, St Malo's corsairs were sponsored by the city's traders and *armateurs* (shipowners) and sanctioned by the state. They carried letters of marque from the Crown which licensed their piracy in return for a share of the spoils.

Training for the priesthood appears to have been a good way to start a career in corsairing, followed by an early escape to sea. Two of St Malo's most famous maritime heroes followed this course, becoming captains of their vessels by the time they were 20. René Duguay-Trouin, born in 1673, was the tearaway son of a rich shipowner who set the piratical pace by capturing or sinking 85 English ships before he was 30. An aristocratic bandit who became chronically melancholic when on land, he was held captive in Plymouth for a year but then escaped by boat. In 1711 he took Rio de Janeiro from the Portugese and the following year quit the seas at the age of 36. This did not prevent him becoming a Lieutenant General in the French Navy, and he died in 1736 garlanded with honours.

Robert Surcouf, born a century later in 1773, graduated from slave-trading to piracy with an early coup, the seizure of the 150-strong HMS *Triton* with a force of only 18 men. His ships hounded the vessels of the East India Company in the Indian Ocean. The crowning exploit of his notorious career occurred in the Bay of Bengal in 1800 when he captured the 26 cannon HMS *Kent* in a famous David and Goliath naval engagement. He too retired at the age of 36. In due course he became a Baron of the French Empire and died in 1827, having become, as a result of his exploits the richest shipowner in France.

2. Cancale

If you like oysters Cancale is the best place to eat them. 11 miles (17.6km) east of St Malo, this modest and respectable port has completely abandoned itself to the cultivation and dégustation of these sensuous bivalves. If you've just arrived and are eager for a taste of Brittany, or if you like to head for home with fond memories, try an oyster lunch in Cancale. Be sure to get there soon after 12pm to ensure a good choice of restaurants, especially at weekends when multitudinous French families turn out for a slap-up meal—come 2pm you could well find it's nigh on impossible to get a table.

Leave St Malo heading east on the coastal road (D201) passing through the suburbs of Paramé to Rothéneuf. For an unusual diversion (20mins) look for a turning left as you pass through the centre of Rothéneuf signposted to **'Les Rochers Sculptés'**. This will take you down to a point in the cliffs where the rocks have been carved into a granite wonderland of faces, figures and creatures by a local priest, Abbé Fouré. He began work in 1870 and laboured for twenty-five years to produce some 300 carvings recounting the history and characters of the Rothéneuf family. Not all have sur-

Les Rochers Sculptés

Granite face, Les Rochers Sculptés

vived the ravages of time and weather, but if you let your eyes adjust to reading the rocks you'll find you're being watched by a lot more stony people than initial appearances suggest.

The D201 continues out to the **Pointe du Grouin**, a well-ventilated headland where the sea is often a truly emerald colour. From here there are panoramic views across the Baie du Mont St Michel to Normandy, the horizon pierced by its famous abbey. Nearby is the Ile des Landes, a bird sanctuary where black cormorants breed.

From Pointe du Grouin it's a short ride down into **Cancale**—turn left into the town centre and park by the church. From here you can walk downhill (rue du Port), past the Tourist Office to the port. Here fish restaurants stretch the length of the quayside with gaggles of lip-licking promenaders inspecting the menus outside.

Choosing where to eat is fun—if you plan to eat oysters and other seafood there's not much between them all, though some are considerably cheaper than others. **Le Nerval** (20 Quai Gambetta. Tel: 99 89 63 12) is a safe bet with *menu fixes* from around 100F which includes a choice of 10 *huîtres creuses* (hollow) or 6 *huîtres farcies* (stuffed). Cancale is also a good place to try a *plateau de fruits de mer* or some local fish such as skate *(raie),* turbot or monkfish *(lotte)*—see the *Dining Experiences* section.

The restaurants here also cater for gourmet tastes with five-course menus from 130F upwards and some death-defying *menu gastronomique* at around 200F. Away from the hoi-polloi **Restaurant de Bricourt** (1 rue du Guesclin. Tel: 99 89 64 76—at the top of the town) is located in an early 19th-century house with a garden and two-Michelin-star cuisine. If you like performance cookery take lots of money and book well ahead. At the other end of the scale you can have an equally regal meal at one of the open-air oyster bars along the port—here a few francs will set you up with a plate of oysters and a *demi-bouteille* of chilled Muscadet, a wine consumed in Cancale in vast quantities.

Cancale's oysters were famous even in Roman times and up until

Pointe du Grouin

Cancale oysters

the 1850s they were simply collected wild from the Baie du Mont St Michel. Their strong flavour is said to derive from the strong tides that wash over them daily. Today they are farmed commercially and if you walk out to the jetty at the eastern end of the port you can see the *parcs* where they are cultivated. Oysters spend four or five years in the water before they arrive on our tables: until the 1960s only flat oysters (*plates*, also known as Bélons) were cultivated here. Then a combination of severe winters and mysterious diseases decimated the population and now hollow oysters *(creuses)*, imported originally from Portugal (known as *portugaises*) but now from Japan (known as *gigas* but still also called *portugaises*) are farmed too.

The beds you can see (or half-see if the tide is in) represent only part of the cultivated area. Cancale oysters actually originate in the Gulf of Morbihan and neighbouring rivers, the year-old spat being brought here to mature in deep-water beds. Later they are moved to shallower waters to be cleansed of mud and impurities—the basins you can see. It's worth walking down to the *parcs* to see the oyster-farmers at work, a hardy bunch whose lives are ruled by the

Oyster culture in Cancale

tide, their cheery faces whipped ruddy by mud, salt and wind. There are also plenty of stalls selling this curious delicacy.

From here you can walk up onto the cliffs above and join the *Sentier des Douaniers* (Customs Officers' Path) that weaves around the coast back to the Pointe du Grouin. A short way along you will come to a small turning to your left (follow the signs to L'Église) which takes you back to the church and car park.

If you want to know more about the strange world of the oyster Cancale has a small local **museum** devoted to the trade housed in the former church of St Méen (open daily July–August and idiosyncratically during rest of year—see Tourist Ofiice window for times). There is also a new **Musée de l'Huître** on the c15 as you head out from the port towards Les Portes Rouges, open July–September, four guided visits daily. If that's not enough a little further round the Baie du Mont St Michel at **Le Vivier-sur-Mer** is France's principal centre for mussel-farming.

Plateau de fruits de mer

3. Dinan

Set high on a hill overlooking the Rance valley, Dinan obligingly fulfills the dream of what a French town should be like. The outskirts may be modern and chaotic but at its heart you'll find a medieval shopping centre lined with half-timbered houses wonky as a pantomime village. With no pressing sights to tax the tourist's conscience visitors are free to wander idly down its cobbled streets, inspecting the mouth-watering charcuteries and pâtisseries and gathering their energy for a lazy boat-trip or gentle riverside walk.

Dinan has all the well-heeled bustle of a market-town which thankfully saves it from becoming too picturesque. Park, if you can, in the large **place du Guesclin** (but not on a Thursday which is market day). Here a statue of Dinan's favourite son, Bertrand du Guesclin, disdainfully surveys the parked cars that now assemble on what was, in his day, a medieval fairground. Ugly and uncouth, Du Guesclin (1321–80) rose to become Constable of France and one of its greatest warriors: his methods were unchivalrous, mercenary and extremely successful—it was he who was mainly responsible for expelling the English from France during the Hundred Years War. In 1359 in the next-door place du Champ he fought and won a single combat duel against the English knight, Thomas of Canterbury.

From the place du Guesclin walk through the rue St Claire, turn-

Dinan

Basilica St Sauveur

ing left by the Tourist Office into the rue de l'Horloge. You are now back in the Middle Ages, all credit cards accepted. Look out for the **Maison du Gisant** which has an arcaded porch beneath which lies a ready-made headless tombstone discovered during restoration. Further on you reach the 15th-century **clock tower**, once the town hall. From the top there are extensive views over Dinan's steep-roofed houses to the surrounding countryside (tower open June–September 10.45am–1.15pm, 3–6pm, but avoid going on the hour unless you want to be deafened by the bells!).

You'll find Dinan's street-names provide a quick guide to how the town once looked. The rue de l'Horloge (Clock Street) soon becomes the place des Merciers (Haberdashers) and then the place des Cordeliers (Franciscan monks). Turn right here down the rue de la Lainerie (Woolshops) then right again along the rue de la Poissonnerie (Fishmongers), from where you can walk via the rue de la Larderie (Baconsellers) to the **Basilica St Sauveur**.

Begun in the 12th century the basilica is refreshingly asymmetrical with a happy marriage of modern and 15th-century stained-glass windows creating a calm, sun-dappled ambience. Along the left-hand side walls you'll find a tombstone containing the heart of du Guesclin. That is all you will find too, for the rest of Dinan's hero is scattered between here and the Languedoc. Following his death in 1380 at Châteauneuf-de-Randon his corpse underwent a macabre return journey. After embalming the entrails were buried at Le Puy

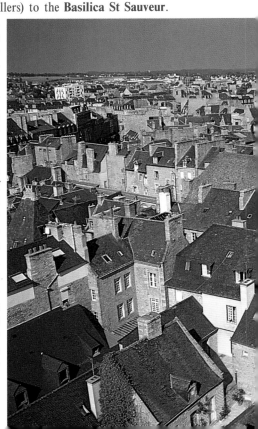

Dinan's rooftops from the clock tower

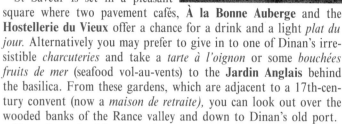

(near Lyon) but this was so poorly done the flesh had to be removed and buried at Montferrand (in the Dordogne), at which point the King intervened and ordered the skeleton be taken to the Basilica St Denis in Paris.

St Saveur is set in a pleasant square where two pavement cafés, **À la Bonne Auberge** and the **Hostellerie du Vieux** offer a chance for a drink and a light *plat du jour.* Alternatively you may prefer to give in to one of Dinan's irresistible *charcuteries* and take a *tarte à l'oignon* or some *bouchées fruits de mer* (seafood vol-au-vents) to the **Jardin Anglais** behind the basilica. From these gardens, which are adjacent to a 17th-century convent (now a *maison de retraite),* you can look out over the wooded banks of the Rance valley and down to Dinan's old port.

From here the itinerary takes you on an easy walk along and beside Dinan's ramparts (45mins)—if you prefer to omit this you can cut back through to the Rue du Jerzual and walk down to the port (see two paragraphs below). To start the walk turn right at the bottom of the Jardin Anglais into the Promenade de la Duchesse Anne, shaded with beech trees. This traces the route of the town's old ramparts, which peter out unhelpfully when you reach the busy rue du General de Gaulle. Continue up the hill till you reach the

Porte St Louis where you can cross over and walk round the 15th-century **Tour de Coëtquen**. This is part of the Château Duchesse Anne which also houses an undemanding **museum** of local history (open June–mid-Oct 10am–6.30pm daily; mid-Mar–May, mid-Oct–mid Nov 10am–12pm, 2–6pm; winter 1.30–5.30pm, closed Tuesdays).

From here you can walk down the Promenade des Petits Fossés with Dinan's massive ramparts for company. Continue past a children's playground (Parc des Petits

Rue de Jerzual

Diables!) to the place Duclos where you can re-enter the old town via the Grand Rue. This leads you past St Malo's **church**, started in the late 15th-century but only completed in 1865, which stands next to the former Franciscan Monastery, now a school.

Grand Rue leads into the rue de la Lainerie then into Dinan's most photogenic street, **rue du Jerzual**. Steep and winding with timbered houses all askew and heavy with geraniums and sagging balconies, this was once the main route into Dinan from the port. Your descent passes through the 14th-century **Jerzual Gate** into the rue du Petit Port, from whence huge loads of cloth made by local weavers were once shipped.

Today **the port** is a quiet backwater mainly used by pleasure craft. If you fancy a quiet jaunt upriver boats can be hired from the **Hôtel Harlequin** across the bridge. To get back to the town you can either walk back up rue du Jerzual or hitch a ride on the *petit train* that frequently passes by. For a longer walk back along the riverside (1hr

30mins) cross the bridge and turn right onto a towpath. The route follows the river round to Léhon where you'll find the ruins of a 17th-century abbey, St Magloire. From here you can climb back up rue Beaumanoir to the Porte St Louis.

For shopping in Dinan try the **Cave des Jacobins** (3 rue St Claire) which provides a good opportunity to pick up some Rance valley cider or some Breton liqueurs. **La Fermette de Menhir** in the place des Cordeliers stocks Breton cheeses. There are also several shops near here selling *faïence* and antiques while **Au Vieux Beffroi** and **Au Rouet** in the rue de l'Horloge both sell *broderie bretonne* and locally-made table linen and lace. Dinan's weaving and craft traditions are continued today by a long parade of crafts shops in rue du Jerzual which sell works in glass, wood, leather and ceramics.

4. Parish Closes

Les enclos paroissiaux are the wonders of Brittany, grandiose religious monuments that will explain Brittany and its people to you far better than any guide book ever can. Most of them are in northern Finistère with a spectacular concentration around the Elorn valley. This itinerary takes you to three of the best: it begins at **St Thégonnec**, a small village 7.4 miles (12km) south-west of Morlaix, which can be reached quickly via the N12 or in a more leisurely way by the D712.

Parish *closes* (walled-in or enclosed areas of hallowed ground) share common characteristics that each village has interpreted in its own way. All are absurdly large for the small rural settlements that surround them, for they were built at a time when Brittany had few urban centres but a disposable wealth derived from maritime trade, flax production and the weaving of cloth. Most were commenced in the mid-16th century and completed in stages over the next two hundred years, elaborate works of devotion born of an intense religious faith and a keen inter-village rivalry.

There are three essential features: a triumphal arch or gateway marking your entry into the sacred ground surrounding the church; a calvary representing scenes from the Passion and Crucifixion, and an ossuary beside the church entrance where bones exhumed from the adjacent cemetery would be housed. These structures are vitalized

St Thégonnec's calvary

and embellished with coarse stone carvings, stern and unyielding granite being the only raw material available for this monumental poetry, now so often movingly reworked by weather. Each ensemble thus achieves several purposes: it serves as a didactic Bible writ large in cartoons of stone, it acts as a tangible bridge of worship between the living and the dead, and it represents a communal act of homage that supercedes the passing of generations.

St Thégonnec

Enter through the **triumphal arch** (1587). To your left is the **ossuary** (1676–82) which is now, inevitably, a depository for postcards and souvenirs. In the **crypt** below is a sepulchral scene depicting Mary Magdalen's sorrow (1702).

Ahead of you rises the **calvary** (1610). Here the craftsmen's work, raised to a humbling but accessible height and silhouetted against

St Thégonnec's triumphal arch

the heavens, sings of the fervent desire of a Breton village to honour the tragedy and serenity of Christ's humiliation. First you see Christ blindfolded and tormented, then (walking anticlockwise) the flagellation, the carrying of the Cross, and finally the Crucifixion. In a niche below this there is a statue of St Thégonnec with a cart pulled by wolves—harnessed up after they devoured his donkey.

The church has a Renaissance **tower** modelled on that at Pleyben with another image of St Thégonnec above the porch. Statues of the Apostles oversee your entry into the nave where the principal attraction is a carved **pulpit** (1683) depicting the Cardinal Virtues. Gaudily painted and lined with busy 18th-century woodcarvings, the interior is typically gloomy in comparison to the simple, animated scenes outside.

Back in lay territory you'll find a couple of *boulangeries* can administer to your bodily needs, while the **Auberge St Thégonnec** (Tel: 98 79 61 18), also a hotel, has an excellent restaurant serving local dishes. When you leave take the D712 towards Kermat, where you turn left for Guimiliau.

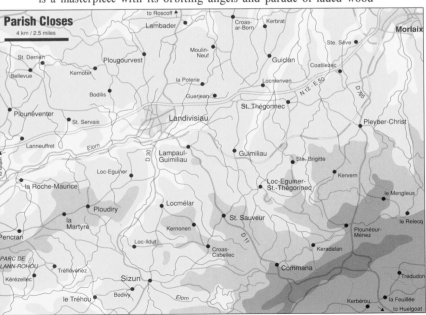

Guimiliau

Here the architecture is on a smaller but even more remarkable and endearing scale. Once more there is a triumphal arch, with a calvary to the right of the church and beyond it a funereal chapel. The **calvary** (1581–8) is the most intense in Brittany, and described with typical Breton severity in the church's companion notes as 'granite with secular lichen'. There are nearly 200 figures adorning it, a lively crowd with billowing moustaches and histrionic grimaces of whom many are wearing 16th-century dress.

The statues are on two levels, the lower section somewhat sober and rigid, the top vigorous and dynamic. Amongst the customary scenes from the Passion (in no chronological order) is a cautionary illustration of a local Breton legend, the torment of Katell Gollet (Catherine the Damned). Katell's crime was to steal a consecrated wafer in order to please her lover (the Devil in disguise), for which she was despatched to Hell to be tortured by demons. Her demise is graphically depicted above the Last Supper, an admonitory warning to all flirtatious women.

The **funereal chapel** (1648) has an exterior pulpit originally used for open-air sermons on All Souls' Day, an occasion that must have made an extraordinary medieval scene. To the left of the church entrance is the ossuary. The church itself, with its leaning tower, looks somewhat unstable—above the porch is a statue of St Miliau, a King of Cornouaille who was beheaded by his evil brother. The **porch** (1606–17), the traditional place of assembly for the parish council, is a masterpiece with its orbiting angels and parade of faded wood-

and stone Apostles. The interior is also rewarding, with a 17th-century organ unsteadily supported by columns and an octagonal carved oak baptistry (1675).

Beyond the church walls the *crêperie* **Ar Chupen** reminds us of more mundane pleasures. Menu-scrutineers will observe that one of its more popular delights is a *crêpe du pagan,* a divine combination of bacon, mushrooms and artichoke hearts.

When you leave take the D111 down the hill to Lampaul-Guimiliau.

Lampaul-Guimiliau

As you near this parish *close* you'll notice the church has a wounded demeanour, the result of a lightning strike which demolished most of its spire in 1809. Enter the close through its monumental gate (1669)—to the left is the chapel and ossuary (1667), to the right a simple calvary.

This time it is the **church**, commenced in 1609, that steals the show. Above the entrance is a statue of St Pol with St Michael below; the **porch** (1533) is guarded by the traditional twelve Apostles. Inside the church the fervid decoration appears to result

from an obsessive desire to carve and paint every available surface. Scenes from the Passion are portrayed along the rood-beam separating the nave from the choir, while on the 17th-century altarpiece the birth of the Virgin Mary and the martyrdom of the headless St Miliau are depicted in painted wood panels. Look out also for the faded gilt banners of St Pol (1634) and the Virgin (1667), now displayed in cases but which are still paraded annually when Lampaul-Guimiliau holds its *pardon.*

More Parish Closes

If you're hooked there's plenty more *enclos paroissiaux* nearby. Travelling anti-clockwise from Lampaul-Guimilau you'll find them at La Roche-Maurice (where there is a threatening

Martyrdom of St Miliau,
Lampaul-Guimiliau

depiction of Ankou, the Breton embodiment of Death), La Martyre (the oldest of them all), Ploudiry, Sizun (which has a magnificent triumphal arch) and Commana. You can also pick up a leaflet from Tourist Offices outlining a *circuit des enclos paroissiaux*. Further afield there are outstanding parish closes at Pleyben (near Châteaulin, one of the largest in Brittany), Plougastel-Doulas (another well-populated calvary) and, surprisingly adrift from all these, a calvary at Guéhenno (near Josselin).

5. Roscoff

Few holiday-makers visited Roscoff before it became a Channel port and there's no need to make a special trip to see it. However if you're one of the 450,000 visitors who catch a ferry here each year you'll find it's a pleasant place to while away some time.

The old port of Roscoff lies to the west of the modern deep-water harbour and ferry terminal. A long seafront curves round the bay with the Tourist Office, housed in a former chapel, bang in the middle. Leading north from here a back street, the rue Gambetta, provides a popular opportunity for some last-minute shopping before heading for home. For local specialities try the *poissonnerie* **Maron** (No. 23), which sells jars of its home-made *soupe de poissons,* while a little further on in rue Amiral Réveillère the *pâtisserie* **Alain Guyader** sells Breton liqueurs, cakes and chocolates. In the same street (No. 1) **Rosko Goz** stocks stripey Breton T-shirts, fishermens'

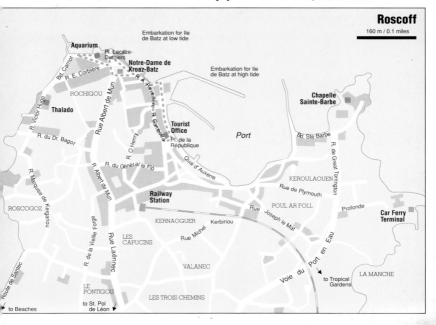

Roscoff old port

sweaters, dufflecoats and sailing gear. There is no hypermarket in Roscoff (the nearest is in Morlaix) but there is a large **Super-U** *supermarché* on the main D789 into town (open Monday–Saturday 9am–7.30pm but closed 12.15–2pm Monday–Friday).

Roscoff's back streets also reveal its history. Rue Amiral Réveillère runs into the triangular place Lacaze Duthiers where a few granite façades remain from the 16th and 17th-century shipowners' mansions that were once a grand feature of the port. Like St Malo, Roscoff has a piratical past and the coast west of here was once notorious for the cliff-top bonfires lit by the locals as false beacons intended to lure foreign ships onto the rocks.

If you look at the thick granite walls of the church **Notre Dame de Kroaz Batz** nearby you'll see cannon bristling from the tower and weather-beaten sailing ships cruising over the porch. The church was begun in 1515 but is still in a Gothic style, architectural fashions, like everything else, taking a long time to reach Finistère. However the lantern belltower (1550–76) has a Renaissance grace. As you enter the church look to your right where there is a Gallo-Roman **font** used for total-immersion baptisms. The unembellished interior still has a 16th-century austerity—its most notable feature is a series of 15th-century alabaster panels depicting the Passion—originally there were seven but three were stolen in 1981.

In the far corner of the place Lacaze Duthiers a narrow street takes you to the fortress-like **Charles Perez Aquarium** which has a collection of over 300 aquatic specimens from the Channel. Other diversions can be found back by the port's main jetty: inevitably a *petit train* offers a tour of the town while Vedettes Blanches run hourly trips to the **Ile de Batz** (see Option 9). On the other side of the ferry terminal the **Tropical Gardens** provide colourful and exotic floral evidence of Roscoff's mild climate while to the west of the old port 'Thalado' offers a free introduc-

General view of Roscoff

**Notre Dame de Kroaz Batz
church porch**

tion to the astonishing world of
seaweed. Roscoff claims to be the
birthplace of thalassotherapy and
has two centres (see *Activities* section, page 107).

The best sandy beach near to
Roscoff is to the west of the old port at **Laber** and there are even
better ones beyond Plouescat. Roscoff is not a place to splash out
on an expensive meal—you'll get better value if you settle yourself
into one of the welcoming cafés and *crêperies* around the old port.
La Brocherie in rue Edouard Corbière (off the place Lacaze
Duthiers) specializes in *brochettes* and if you like big old seaside
hotels try the cavernous seaview restaurant in the **Hôtel des Arcades**
(15 rue Amiral Réveillère).

6. Quimper

'A charming little place' Flaubert called Quimper, and it's hard
to disagree. Founded by St Corentin some time between the 4th
and 7th-centuries, the city developed around the confluence of the
Steir and Odet rivers to become the ancient capital of Cornouaille.
Today it's Brittany's most Celtic city where specialist shops sell
traditional costumes, keltia musique and Breton-language books.

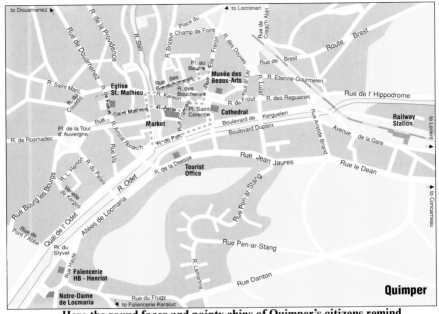

Quimper

Here the round faces and pointy chins of Quimper's citizens remind one of their Welsh and Cornish ancestors, a heritage that is celebrated proudly every July with a great Celtic shindig, the Fêtes de Cornouaille.

Quimper sprawls, an endearing feature that contributes to its relaxed and unpretentious atmosphere. If you're coming from the north try to park near the church of St Mathieu in the rue de Falkirk. From here it's a short walk down rue St Mathieu to the pedestrianized sanctuary of Vieux Quimper. If you arrive in the morning make straight for the **Halles St François** (straight ahead), a covered market open Monday to Saturday. Quimper's old market burnt down in 1976 and its replacement is a bright, airy building with huge roof-beams like an inverted boat. Look out for a stall (P Capitaine) selling honey and *hydromel* from Quéménéven and be sure

to visit a *boulangerie* here to buy yourself *cent grammes de feuilletés aux fromage,* flaky pastry cheese straws.

From the market you can turn left up rue St François into the main shopping street, rue Kéréon, then walk right towards Quimper's imposing cathedral, **St Corentin**. It dates from 1240 but has been ceaselessly altered ever since. Unfortunately its most interesting feature (the choir stands at an unusual angle to the nave) can't be seen at present as most of the cathedral has been closed off for a four-year period of restoration (begun in January 1990). The exterior craftily conceals this deviance but you will be able to spot a statue of King Gradlon on horseback set between the two spires of the west front. **King Gradlon** is Quimper's mythical founder who

Café du Finistère; King Gradlon

was forced to move here after the Devil tricked his wayward daughter into flooding his kingdom, Ys, now a drowned city in the Bay of Douarnenez.

Around the cathedral and the place St Corentin there are often stalls selling lace and Breton souvenirs; in one corner of the square you'll find the **Café du Finistère**, a good meeting point where you can sit and watch the Quimperois go by. Nearby you'll see a statue of René Laënnec (1781–1826), inventor of the stethoscope. It stands outside the excellent **Musée des Beaux Arts** which houses a small, feet-friendly collection of European paintings and drawings from the 16th-century onwards (open 9.30am–noon, 2–6pm, closed Tuesdays).

Apart from the outstanding quality of many of the works its most interesting aspect is the historical insight it offers into Breton life. Here you can still find that romantic, mystical Brittany of popular imagination which is probably half the reason so many people come to the region—a Bretagne of bustling markets and back-breaking toil in the fields, of lonely calvaries and solemn *pardons,* stormy seascapes and sacred woods. The collection is strongest in late 19th and early 20th-century works (the Pont-Aven school is well represented) but it also introduces refreshingly modern Quimper-born artists such as Pierre de Belay and Max Jacobs. Don't miss it.

Quimper's other main attractions are shopping, café-hopping and *faïence.* For shopping venture up the rue Élie Fréron into Vieux Quimper, a network of quiet streets with small designer boutiques and shops selling antiques and *brocante.* Look out for **No. 8** in this street where you can buy all the pans and utensils to start your own mini-*crêperie* when you get home. The proprietor will even give you

Vieux Quimper

Hand-painted faïence

some recipes to start you off and the shop also sells cider bowls and jugs. From here you can cut left through to the rue des Gentilshommes and back down to the river. For Breton music try **Keltia Musique** in the place au Buerre while **Bijoux Bretons** in the rue du Parc sells locally made jewellery including Celtic-inspired designs in beaten silver by Toul Hoat.

The rue du Parc is also where you'll find two of Quimper's more upmarket riverside (and traffic-side) cafés, the **Café de l'Épée** and the **Grande Café de Bretagne**. The latter is also a *brasserie* where you can eat on a scale to suit your appetite. Quimper is not really a place for lavish dining but one for snacks and cheap meals—have an omelette here and a *plat du jour* there—you'll find more bars and restaurants if you wend your way towards the railway station or go across the river towards the allées de Locmaria. The city is also one of the few places in Brittany where having a *crêpe* and some *cidre* seems the natural thing to do and not just some fast-food for tourists. The **Crêperie au Vieux Quimper** (20 rue Verdelet, closed Tuesdays) is one of the most popular and there are more good *crêperies* in the place au Beurre. For a cheap no-nonsense, no-frills steak and chips try **Chez Françoise** nearby (12, rue Élie Fréron).

For *faïence*, Quimper's distinctive pottery, two shops have good selections: **Art de Cornouaille** (12, place St Corentin) and **La Civette** (16 bis, rue du Parc). It is not cheap (from 400F upwards for a large plate) but nearby factories sell seconds, and you can take a guided tour (30mins) around the workshops.

Faïence has been made in Quimper since 1690. The pottery was originally produced to meet local needs, for example as wedding presents and heirlooms, but now it exports it to collectors all over the world. Today machinery is used to make the pottery but the designs are still hand-painted, the decoration being applied to the piece before the final firings. The nearest factory is HB-Henriot, just across from the church Notre Dame de Locmaria (open March–October, tours Monday–Friday, 9.30–11.30am, 1.30–4.30pm, except Friday 1.30–3pm). Another is the smaller **Faïenceries Kéraluc** which produces a more modern design of *faïence*. This is a little further along the Bénodet road at 14 rue de la Troménie (open Monday–Saturday 9am–noon, 2–6pm; low season Monday–Friday only, closes at 5pm).

HB-Henriot faïence factory sign

Stone alignments, Carnac

7. Carnac

Considering that Carnac is one of the world's great prehistoric sites it comes as a surprise to many visitors just how casually its ancient treasures are displayed. According to the local council there are exactly 2,792 menhirs (standing-stones) protruding from the heathland to the north of this seaside town. Most of them are in neat, parallel rows (alignements) that stretch for over 2 miles (3.8km), erected by a highly organized and industrious race anytime between 4000 and 1800BC. Until recently visitors were free to walk, climb and picnic around these perplexing megaliths which some will find a source of apoplectic delight and others dismiss as diminutive and disappointing. Now, perhaps several millennia too late, efforts are being made to protect them.

Certain steps can make your visit to Carnac considerably more meaningful. Firstly if you're approaching from the north try to arrive via minor roads, taking the D186 south (which you can join at Kergroix) till you reach the D196, where you turn right along the **'Route des Alignements'** to Carnac. This back route provides the most dramatic introduction to the megaliths—it may be crawling with traffic but the slower you go the longer you'll get to see the stones.... Coming this way you will pass three main groups—the Alignements de Kerlescan (the least visited), the Alignements de Kermario (the

Megaliths, Carnac

67

What Are All These Stones Doing Here?

Wandering amongst the menhirs of Carnac one soon appreciates the precision with which these immense stones have been placed. Whoever erected them had a clear purpose, a high degree of engineering skill and a huge workforce. Similar megalithic structures have been found throughout Europe but never in such numbers or in such a large-scale pattern as here.

History has not helped us in our puzzling. It is clear that once there were many more stones here, perhaps even twice as many. Erosion, earthquakes and man's pillaging have all disfigured the original design, with stones being destroyed by builders, removed by farmers and repositioned by well-intentioned but amateur archaeologists. Not that this has prevented hundreds of experts from finding pattern in their madness. Close surveying and statistical analysis has now made it clear that the alignments have a thoroughness of design not readily apparent to the eye of the casual visitor. The menhirs are not spaced equally, but grow closer together towards their outer rows. At the same time the rows converge fan-like as they move eastwards, and the size of the individual stones increases. Sometimes the rows take a bend northwards, sometimes they are not rows but parallel curves. All this could imply a central axis, and indeed one has been nominated, the Grand Menhir at Locmariaquer. Perhaps all the megaliths scattered around Morbihan were part of a large network designed, say, to plot the movements of the moon and stars.

Many people feel that the alignments do form part of some primitive calculator, perhaps for recording or deducing astronomical data, perhaps simply as a diary for the seasons to aid farmers. Others attribute a deeper religious significance: perhaps the stones are an act of worship, a message from the living to the dead, or a zodiac temple. Folklore offers other suggestions: the stones, phallic-shaped and erected at angles, were part of fertility rituals in which, anointed with honey, wax and oil, they became restorative slides for barren women. Perhaps they were part of annual communal festivals, with a new stone erected each year to the light of nocturnal ritual fires and sacrificial ceremonies. This might explain why over the centuries many Christians have called for the destruction of the stones, and why elsewhere they have been capped with crosses. Or maybe it doesn't. Perhaps Flaubert is the only man to have got it right so far. 'Carnac' he declared, 'has had more rubbish written about it than it has standing stones.'

Standing stones, Carnac

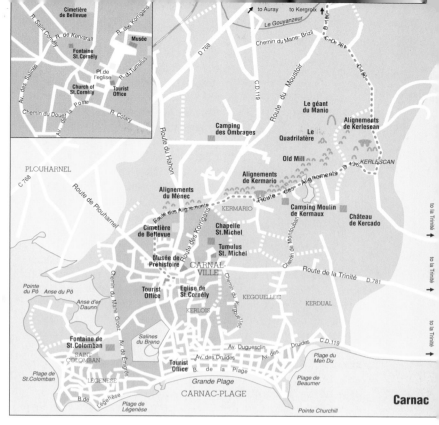

largest and most impressive) and, after you have crossed the D119, the Alignements de Ménec.

Secondly the best time to visit these sites is dawn or dusk: if you're staying in Carnac it's well worth popping back for a pre-dinner stroll for at such half-lit times the menhirs take on an eery, even spooky mood, stretching into the night like massed tombstones. If this is impractical then you may be lucky and hit a lull when everyone else is at lunch. It's best to take a good long walk up and down the lines, or better still hire a bicycle from Lorcy, 6 rue de Courdiec, Carnac-Ville (closed Mondays) or a horse from the Centre Équestre des Menhirs at Camping de la Grande Métaire.

Finally pay a visit to the **Musée de Préhistoire** in the place de la Chapelle centre (open all year 10am–noon, 2–6pm (5pm winter), closed Tuesdays September–June). This is a far from dull affair which sets Carnac's megaliths into the context of prehistory in an ignoramus-friendly way. Many of the contents excavated from the tumuli and dolmens in the area are displayed here including some hauntingly beautiful primitive stone carvings. Explanatory booklets in English can be borrowed and the collection extends right up to the colonization of Brittany by the Romans and Celts.

If you get the megalith bug the museum has also has a useful bookshop with guides to the other 3,000 menhirs, dolmens and tumuli

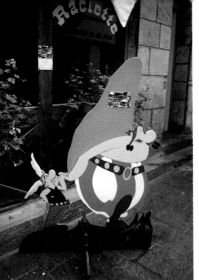

Asterix, popular Celtic cartoon hero

dotted around Morbihan. **Locmariaquer** nearby is another principal site where you can inspect 'Le Grand Menhir', the world's largest standing stone (64ft, 20.3m) which is now, alas, broken into four pieces. Masochists may also care to take a short guided journey into the interior of the extensive **Tumulus de St Michel** to the east of Carnac (open 10am–noon, 2-5pm). It was probably erected around 3,000BC and like all graves is dark, smelly and claustrophobic inside. From the top, where a modern chapel has been built, there are reasonable views of the surrounding region and very good ones of the Hôtel Tumulus's washing.

Carnac itself is divided into two parts: Carnac-Ville and Carnac-Plage. The **beach** here is a good long stretch of pale sand, one of the best in the area and therefore well-attended. On the hill above it Carnac-Ville radiates out from the traffic-throttled church of **St Cornély**, which has an eye-catching baroque stone canopy above its north entrance. The church is dedicated to St Cornelius, patron saint of horned animals and it's worth venturing inside to see the scenes from his life painted on the central wooden vaults of the ceiling in the 1730s by an artist from Pontivy.

In medieval times Carnac was the focus of an important week-long *pardon* when all the local cattle would be brought to the church to be blessed—just downhill from the Pâtisserie Le Rolle in rue St Cornély you can still see an 18th-century fountain used for this purpose. St Cornély inveighed against the pagan practice of animal sacrifice and was martyred for his views by the Romans. Legend says that the legionaries chased him and his two oxen all the way from Rome to Carnac. On reaching the sea he turned upon his pursuers furiously and transformed them to stone; these petrified warriors have puzzled archaeologists ever since.

In Carnac-Ville the **Tourist Office** in the place d'Église (open April–September) has maps and leaflets detailing short walks in the vicinity of Carnac. There is another office in Carnac-Plage (74, avenue des Druides) open all year. The **Hôtel Marine**, 4 place la Chapelle, Tel: 97 52 07 33 (closed January–February), in Carnac-Ville has a brasserie and a restaurant and therefore caters for all needs with lo-

Church of St Cornély

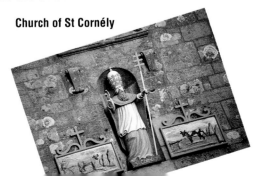

cal seafood a principal feature of its menus. The modern bar, shaped like an upturned boat, is clean, lively and popular with locals. **Le Râtelier** (4 chemin du Douët. Tel: 97 52 05 04), also a hotel, has a quieter, country-house ambience with excellent food but slow service (closed Oct–Nov).

8. Vannes

If you arrive here after touring round western Brittany, where life is perpetually sensible and conservative, then Vannes will come as a welcome surprise. Being that bit closer to the body of France the city has a lively Gallic energy in keeping with its status as a former capital of the region. Today it is a busy agricultural and industrial centre with all the horrendous development on the city outskirts this implies, but at its centre you'll find one of the most enjoyable old towns in Brittany.

If you're coming from the north try to park in the place de la République in the rue Thiers. Today this long street, which runs north-south, marks the western edge of the old town with the remnants of Vannes' medieval ramparts bordering the east. As you drive down rue Thiers you won't be able to miss the imposing **Hôtel de Ville**, built in the 1880s and defended by an equestrian statue of Arthur de Richemont, the Breton Duke who defeated the English at the end of the Hundred Years War.

From the place de la République it's a short walk south to the Tourist Office, operating from a 17th-century town house known as the **Hôtel de Limur** (open June–September), and thence round to Vannes' picturesque Port de Plaisance. Here the **Porte St Vincent** (1704) marks the traditional gateway into the medieval town from the port, once a bustling harbour but now a canalised *cul-de-sac* frequented by pleasure craft. The pavement cafés in the adjacent place Gambetta offer a comfortable vantage point for watching Vannes go by.

Leave the place Gambetta and continue east round the side of the city walls and along the rue Le Pontois. The road runs beside Vannes' impressive ramparts, now well-restored but still containing parts of

71

**Left, Vannes' ramparts.
Right, the medieval quarter.
Below, 17th-century washhouses.**

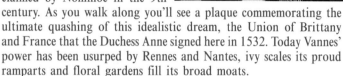

the city walls constructed by the Romans in the 4th century. Vannes gets its name from the Veneti, the Celtic tribe whose sailing ships dominated the Gulf of Morbihan up until a windless day in 56BC when a fleet of oar-propelled galleys commanded by Julius Caesar destroyed them.

It was from Vannes that the Romans built their roads penetrating into all parts of Armorica. Later the city became the capital of the first Breton kingdom, proclaimed by Nominoë in the 9th century. As you walk along you'll see a plaque commemorating the ultimate quashing of this idealistic dream, the Union of Brittany and France that the Duchess Anne signed here in 1532. Today Vannes' power has been usurped by Rennes and Nantes, ivy scales its proud ramparts and floral gardens fill its broad moats.

For a better view of the ramparts and the medieval town beyond you can cross the road and climb up to the Promenade de la Garenne, which rejoins the rue Le Pontois a little further on. If you continue on the lower level you'll soon come to the **Porte Poterne**, where beneath the bridge there are some picturesque 17th-century washhouses. Further on you'll pass the 15th-century Constable's Tower and then the 16th-century Powder Tower. The grand building to your right is the Préfecture, built in the 1880s.

Carry on past this till you meet the small Porte Prison which leads into the old town. Climbing up the hill veer to the right, round the back of the Cathédrale St Pierre, along rue des Chanoines (canons) into the place Henri IV. Now you are in the centre of Vannes' *quartier médiéval,* a subtly restored confusion of cobbled streets and lop-

Half-timbered houses in the medieval quarter

sided half-timbered houses where for once the carefully inserted banks and designer shops do not deaden the authentic ring of history. As it happens the most incongruous building here turns out to be the over-sized **Cathédrale St Pierre**, a veritable jigsaw of styles that architects have been fiddling with since the 13th century.

Inside the porch to the left you'll find a colour-coded plan revealing just what a jumble of ideas the place is. No doubt this makes it a godsend to lecturers in the history of ecclesiastical architecture but for the casual visitor only the Chapel of the Holy Sacrament (fourth *chapelle* on your left) is essential viewing. This contains the tomb of Vincent Ferrier, the Spanish saint to whom the cathedral is dedicated. Born in Valencia in 1350, St Vincent was a Dominican monk who spent a peripatetic life preaching all over Europe, arriving in Vannes only a year before his death in 1419. Such was his popularity that its citizens refused both the Dominican and Spanish claims on his body, voting to restore their cathedral as a fitting home for his grave which had since become a fount-head of miracles.

Opposite the entrance to the cathedral stands a former covered market and courthouse known as **La Cohue** (the throng or hub-bub). Many parts of the building date from the 13th century, which was also used as a theatre until 1940. Now it houses the **Musée de La Cohue**, an imaginatively displayed collection of art and artefacts relevant to the history of Vannes and past life in the Gulf of Morbihan (open daily 14 June–15 September 10am–6pm, rest of the year 10am–noon, 2–6pm closed Tuesdays and Sundays).

Walk through La Cohue to the rue des Halles, where you will find a useful delicatessen called **La Taste**. This stocks a good range of Breton specialities, including the local *chouchen*. From here follow rue des Halles south into the place Valencia where, from beneath the eaves of a 16th-century house, jut a merry couple carved in wood called, 'Vannes and his wife'.

Around the corner in the rue Noë is the **Musée d'Archéologie** housed in the 15th-century Château Gaillard, once the seat of the Breton parliament. The museum contains finds from the megalithic sites in Morbihan including jewellery from Carnac and Locmariaquer (open daily April–September 9.30am–noon, 2–6pm, rest of the year Monday–Friday 2–5.30pm).

From the place Valencia take the narrow rue de les Orfèvres (gold-smiths) back to the rue de la Monnaie. On the corner look out for the bright apricot decor of the **Pâtisserie R Loysance**, a genteel *salon de thé* where you should try—or take away *(à emporter)*—some *kouign amann,* the *spécialité de la maison* and the most delicious of the Breton sticky cakes.

Walk down the rue de la Monnaie into the place des Lices (lists), once a field where medieval tournaments were held. On Wednesday and Saturday mornings a general market is held here and in the nearby place du Poids Public, with a separate fish market in the place de la Poissonnerie. Further downhill the rue St Vincent leads you back through the Porte St Vincent to the place Gambetta.

For eating out Vannes has plenty to offer its visitors though within the old city walls prices can be steep. The *crêperie* **Le Sarrazin**, 16 rue des Vierges, has a terrace with views from the ramparts. Down by the left bank of the port (rue F le Dressay) **Le Brick** has an upstairs restaurant offering basic fare for hungry yachtsmen and women. For something upmarket venture up the rue de la Fontane (near the Église St Paterne) to **La Morgate** which specialises in seafood (Tel: 97 42 42 39).

For entertainment a mile (1.6km) south from the Port de Plaisance is the **Parc du Golfe**, a leisure complex with one of the largest bowling alleys in France. There is also a **Butterfly Conservatory** and an **Aquarium**. Nearby is the embarkation point for the **Vedettes Vertes** that tour the Gulf of Morbihan (see Option 11 in the *Excursions* section).

Place Valencia, 'Vannes and his wife'

EXCURSIONS...

9. Islands

Brittany's jagged coast is dotted with islands. Most are small granite lumps inhabited by stubborn plants and visited only by seagulls, but there are a few spectacular exceptions. Some of these are only a stone's throw from the shore, like the island of Grand Bé off St Malo which at low tide can be reached by a short walk across the sands. Others are isolated rocks lost in the fogs and storms of the Atlantic, like the Ile d'Ouessant, France's most westerly point. Some are flat and austere but others have beaches, hotels and an unexpectedly bucolic air.

Fifteen are large enough to seduce a permanent population into living on them and you should try to visit at least one of these during your stay. It's true that there's not always a great deal to see when you get there, but the sea crossing is reason enough to go with its chance to look back at the rocky coast of the mainland and watch the seabirds careering round the skies. In the summer months making the crossing to most of the islands is simply a matter of turning up at a quay and boarding the next boat. If the weather's good take a picnic so you can avoid the crowds and inflated prices.

The **Ile de Bréhat** is one of the easiest islands to visit. It's also one of the most charming and could easily be incorporated into your

Island ferry

Fort National, off St Malo

travels along the Côte de Granit Rose (see Day 2 Itinerary). It lies to the north of Paimpol and the embarkation point for the 15-minute crossing is the Pointe de l'Arcouest. The island, which is only 3½km (2.2 miles) long, is really two, linked by a bridge known as the Pont ar Prad. The climate is surprisingly mild allowing oleander, mimosa and a variety of fruit trees to flourish in the gardens and hedges that border its low, undulating fields.

Bréhat has a slightly comic air, like a rural Toytown, for cars are banned and the only ton-up vehicles permitted are baby tractors. Numerous small paths criss-cross the island allowing visitors to lose themselves with ease—be sure to climb up to the **Chapelle Saint-Michel** for a view of the whole island. You could easily spend a pleasant hour or an idle day on Bréhat (there are three hotels, often fully booked) but try to avoid going in the height of summer when it can get overwhelmed with tourists. If you push on to the north island things will be quieter. Bicycles can be hired from the main harbour, **Port Clos**, from where you can also take a one-hour boat tour round the island. Les Vedettes de Bréhat operate crossings to the island from Pointe de l'Arcouest all year (from 8am–7.30pm in July and August), tele-

Sea crossing

Ile de Bréhat

phone: 96 55 86 99. Further information from the Tourist Office in Le Bourg, telephone: 96 20 04 15.

Further west, to the north of Roscoff the **Ile de Batz** is a similar size to Bréhat but sparser, treeless and more windswept. A 20-minute crossing from the mainland, it is still warmed by the Gulf Stream and a mild climate allows the islanders to cultivate small fields of vegetables. Seaweed has long been harvested here—originally for fuel, now for fertilizer. There are two hotels, some sandy beaches and the opportunity for easy-going walks. The company Vedettes Blanche de l'Ile de Batz runs boats to the island from the old port at Roscoff all year (from 8am–8pm July to September), with different embarkation points according to the tides, tel: 98 61 79 66.

Getting to the **Ile d'Ouessant** (also known as Ushant), 18.6 miles (30km) west of the Brest peninsula, can be a rougher experience. Its hazardous waters are where the oil tanker Torrey Canyon went down in 1967, and the beam of its lighthouse at Créac'h, signalling the entrance to the English Channel, is one of the strongest in the world. The crossing takes one-and-a-half hours from Le Conquet and two-and-a-half hours from Brest, from where you can also fly (15 mins with Finist'Air, telephone: 98 84 64 87).

Ouessant is stormy and windswept in winter, besieged by migrating birds in spring and autumn, pleasantly mild in summer. As part of the Parc Regional d'Armorique it is a bird-watcher's paradise and has two interesting sights: the **Eco-musée d'Ouessant**, where two 18th and 19th-century houses have been restored complete with painted

Rockpools, Ile de Bréhat

Chapelle Saint-Michel, Ile de Bréhat

driftwood furniture, and the **Musée des Phares**, a lighthouse museum (both open daily 10.30am–6.30pm June–September, rest of the year April–May 2–6.30pm, October–March 2–4pm, closed Mondays). There are hotels and a campsite. For the Tourist Office tel: 98 48 85 83. Ferries sail to Ouessant daily leaving early in the morning, for times contact the Service Maritime Départemental, telephone: 98 80 24 68. Some boats call in at the small but inhabited island of Molène en route.

The **Ile de Sein**, 5 miles (8km) west of the Pointe du Raz, is only just an island. Its bare, flat landscape rarely rises above 5ft (1½m) and in the past it has almost been submerged. Today some 500 people struggle resolutely to live there, supporting themselves by fishing and gardening in small stone-walled plots. If you're searching for that bleak mystical Brittany ravaged by wind, sea and superstition then Sein may be able to help you. There is one hotel. Boats leave from Audierne year round and take 1hr 15mins—in summer there are several sailings, in winter only one in the morning (not Wednesdays); for details contact the Service Maritime Départemental, telephone: 98 70 02 38.

Island cottages

The southern coast of Brittany is less harsh and its off-shore islands of a correspondingly gentler disposition. **Les Iles de Glénan**, 11 miles (18km) due south of Concarneau, is an archipelago of tiny islands that encircle a tranquil inland sea called 'La Chambre'. Some of its smaller islands are bird reserves but there are no permanent inhabitants. In summer there is a sailing and diving school in operation. Most tourist boats, some would say far too many, call at the northern isle of St Nicholas. The crossing takes 1hr 30mins if you sail from Loctudy, Bénodet, Beg-Meil or Concarneau and you can also depart from Port-la-Forêt (near Fouesnant) or Quimper. Sailings are only in the summer months. Details from Vedettes L'Odet, telephone: 98 57 00 58.

The **Ile de Groix**, a 45-minute crossing from Lorient, is a large flat island with steep cliffs 5 miles (8km) long. Some 2,500 people live there and many seem to rely on the influx of summer tourists to keep them going. There are sandy beaches to the east, two hotels, an Eco-musée and bicycles for hire. It is possible to take a car there—for details of sailings call Compagnie Morbihannaise de Navigation, telephone: 97 21 03 97, or the island Tourist Office, telephone: 97 86 53 08.

Brittany's largest island is also its most southerly, **Belle-Ile**; it covers some 32 square miles (84 square km) and has many attractions to justify the 40-minute crossing from Quiberon. Compared to the other Breton islands it has a rare scenic variety with exposed highlands, sheltered valleys, rugged cliffs and golden beaches. Belle-Ile has a historical and cultural pedigree too—Alexander Dumas set part of *The Three Musketeers* on the island (echoing real events that took place), and the citadelle in its principal town, Le Palais, re-designed by Vauban in the 17th century, was once a prison whose guests included Karl Marx and the son of the Haitian revolutionary Toussaint L'Ouverture. Sarah Bernhardt also lived here in flamboyant style and Flaubert, Monet, Proust and Matisse all stayed on the island.

Today Belle-Ile lives by tourism. It's an impressive island ideal for walking, cycling and exploring; there are several hotels and many campsites. In summer sailings to the island are plentiful and you can take cars; ferries leave the Quiberon peninsula at Port Maria (expect long delays driving up and down the peninsula at weekends and peak times). For reservations contact Compagnie Morbihannaise de Navigation, telephone: 97 31 80 01. You can also sail from Vannes and La Trinité with Navix tel: 97 46 60 00, or fly (15 mins with Insul 'Air from Lorient, tel: 97 31 41 14). For Tourist Information on the island tel: 97 31 81 93.

Plage Bonaparte

10. Beaches

Brittany has some of the best beaches in France. They seem to get bigger and better the more you travel round the region: even at the height of summer, when those in the most popular resorts are as packed with bodies as is decently possible, there is still enough sand to go round. They have variety too, and can cater for all our seaside fantasies—six-course family picnics, intrepid shrimp-hunting expeditions, existential movies starring lone man and a dog. Furthermore, unlike the beaches of the Mediterranean, they do not fail us if the sun disappears: out comes la batte de cricket and the boule, the kites, sand buggies and horses.

These beaches do have drawbacks. One is that if the tide's out the mud's in, and it can be a long, long walk to find the sea. Seaweed can sometimes mar the scene too, making the rocks slippery and walking treacherous. The water is never that warm either, with average sea temperatures only rising to 16° or 17°C (61° or 62°F) at the end of August.

The best beaches are to be found along the northern and southern coasts. One indication of their merit is the award of a Blue Flag from the EC-sponsored Foundation for Environmental Education in Europe. Those marked (BF) in the following guide have been awarded a Blue Flag, showing that they met the minimum levels for bathing water quality set by the EC. An easy way of determining whether they're still up to scratch when you arrive is to see if the flag's still flying.

Golden sands on the Côte d'Emeraude

North Coast

Here a bunting of classic seaside resorts strings along the coast, all of which owe their long-standing popularity to the quality of their beaches. On the Côte d'Emeraude, Dinard is the most elegant of them all, its beach at St Enogat both chic and cheerful. There are also good family beaches backed up by busy resorts at St Cast-le-Guildo, St Jacut-de-la-Mer and St Quay-Portrieux.

On the Côte de Granit Rose the sinuous resort of Perros-Guirec (BF) has an extremely popular plage at Trestraou and a quieter one at Trestrignel. That of nearby Trégastel is famous for the anthropomorphic shapes of its pink granite rocks and there are other fine beaches at Trévou-Tréguignec (BF) and Trébeurden.

For wide expanses of sand with adequate but less overwhelming facilites try (going west) the beaches at Lancieux, Sables d'Or-les-Pins, Erquy, Le Val-André, Binic, Étables-sur-Mer (BF), and, on the other side of the Côte de Granit Rose, the superb stretch at St Michel-en-Grève (BF).

For small out-of-town beaches where you must cater for yourself try those tucked beside the D201 as you head west from St Malo to Pointe du Grouin, or those along the D34A on the Lande de Fréhel (west of Cap Fréhel) such as that at Pléhérel. There is also a small beach north of Paimpol near Ploubazlanec, and another further west at Port Blanc.

In northern Finistère there are well-kept beaches at Carantec and Roscoff but for something more remote you'll have to take yourself off to those on the Ile de Batz. Still further west there are three good beaches near Plouescat and several more at Brignogan Plages.

Walking the dog

Dogs are forbidden on beaches in summer

West Coast

Here the Breton coast turns wild. The shoreline is generally rocky and exposed with waters that are too dangerous for swimming. Nevertheless sheltered sandy beaches can be found, such as the long curl of sand beside Morgat. There are also acceptable beaches at Plougastel-Daoulas (BF), Camaret, Douarnenez (Les Sables Blancs most notably) and in the nearby resort of Tréboul.

South Coast

Bénodet has one of the best beaches in Cornouaille and a great number of visitors to prove it. You may prefer to explore the dunes and coves around Beg-Meil or visit the beaches near Fouesnant and La Forêt-Fouesnant.

East from Lorient there is a long stretch of straight beaches as you head down towards the Presqu'île de Quiberon, most pleasantly at Etel and Erdeven. Quiberon can boast some of the nicest beaches along the south coast but they are often packed and access to them all but impossible on summer weekends. Carnac-Plage nearby is a better bet, or Locmariaquer further east; those in the know take the boat across to Belle-Ile where there are good beaches around Bangor.

North coast beach park

Water is a ubiquitous feature of the Breton landscape and messing about on it an extremely popular activity. As well as a seaboard stretching for some 750 miles (1,207km) Brittany also has 403 miles (650km) of navigable rivers and canals. During the season taking to the boats is *de règle* and you should be sure to join in—leaflets advertising the numerous boat trips available during these summer months are widely available in travel agents and Tourist Offices.

Sea Trips
If you like a voyage with an objective then you should take a day trip to one of the wild or gentle islands lying off the Breton main-land—see Option 9. There are also plenty of opportunities to cruise along the coast. From the Cale de la Bourse in **St Malo** or the Port

Taking to the boats

de Plaisance in **Dinard** Emeraude Lines (Tel: 99 40 48 40) operate trips to Les Iles Chausey (1hr 45mins one way), the Ile de Cézembre (20mins), Cap Fréhel (2hrs 30mins) and around the Baie de St Malo (1hr). For a quick breath of sea air you can take their frequent ferry crossing from St Malo to Dinard (10mins). If you're feel-ing homesick they and Condor (Tel: 99 56 42 29) both offer day trips to Jersey, Guernsey and Sark.

You can also tour the Baie du Mont St Michel for a day or half-day on a wheeled boat, the Sirène de la Baie, either depart-ing direct from Le Vivier-sur-Mer (Tel: 99 48 82 30) or from St Malo through Les Couriers Bretons (Tel: 99 56 79 09). The Association Bisquine Cancalaise run trips in an authentic replica of a *bisquine,* a local three-mast-ed fishing boat; details from their office on the quay at Cancale, Tel: 99 89 77 87. All these trips can be booked in the travel agents next to the Tourist Office in the Esplanade St Vincent.

Birdwatchers should consider the 3-hour round trip from **Perros-Guirec** to the seabird sanctuary at Les Sept Iles which includes a stop on the Ile aux Moines. It's run by Les Vedettes Blanches (Tel:

98 61 76 98) who also offer half-day trips in the Baie de Morlaix from Roscoff. Les Vedettes de Bréhat run full-day sea cruises departing from **Erquy**, **Le Val-André**, **Port Dahouët**, **Binic** and **St Quay-Portrieux** that call at the Ile de Bréhat, bookable through the Tourist Offices in those ports.

Vedettes de Bréhat sea cruise

From the port at **Morgat** on the Crozon peninsula Vedettes Rosmeur (Tel: 98 27 10 71) run 45-minute trips out to the sea-caves and grottoes of the nearby cliffs as well as to the Cap de la Chèvre (2hrs); in July and August they also run trips around the Baie de Douarnenez from **Douarnenez.**

From **Vannes** there are numerous trips to the Gulf of Morbihan, a 46 square-mile (119 square-km) inland sea peppered with small islands. Two of the largest, the Ile d'Arz and the Ile aux Moines are served by frequent ferries from Conleau and Port Blanc respectively. A more luxurious way to travel is by the pleasure cruisers of Les Vedettes Vertes—Navix (Tel: 97 46 46 00) which embark from the Gare Maritime a mile (1.6km) south of Vannes towards Conleau. Their boats circulate between these two islands and Locmariaquer (Tel: 97 57 36 78), Port Navalo (Tel: 97 53 74 12), Le Bono (Tel: 97 57 90 64), Auray (Tel: 97 56 59 47), and La Trinité-sur-Mer (97 55 81 00). Vedettes Angélus operate similar trips from the Port du Guilvin in Locmariaquer (Tel: 97 26 31 35).

Another interesting excursion is to take a boat from Larmor-Baden across to the island of Gavrinis where there is a world-famous tumulus with extraordinary linear carvings on its granite slabs. These are run by Vedettes Blanches Armor, Tel: 97 57 15 27, and sometimes continue with a visit to the Ile aux Moines.

River Trips

The tides determine the pace of trips up the **Rance** to Dinan. These are operated from St Malo and Dinard by Emeraude Lines (Tel: 99 40 48 40) with trips upriver normally taking 2hrs 30mins with bus connection back later (45mins).

Les Vedettes de Bréhat offer half-day cruises up the **Trieux** from the Pointe de l'Arcouest (Tel: 96 55 86 99).

Vedettes L'Odet run round trips up the wooded banks of the **Odet** to Quimper from Bénodet (2hrs 30mins), Loctudy (3hrs 30mins), Beg-Meil (4hrs), Port-la-Forêt and Concarneau (both 4hrs 30mins).

Placid waterways

Lunch or dinner is available on some sailings. With frequent trips in July and August between Quimper and Bénodet, you have the chance to spend most of the day in one of these resorts. For reservations in Quimper telephone: 98 52 98 41; Bénodet telephone: 98 57 00 58; Loctudy telephone: 98 87 45 63; Beg-Meil telephone: 98 94 97 94; Concarneau telephone: 98 50 72 12. Vedettes Glenan also run half-day trips from Concarneau up the Odet (Tel: 98 97 10 31).

Les Vedettes Vertes travel from the outskirts of Vannes up the **Auray** valley to Le Bono and Auray (Tel: 97 47 10 78).

Canal Trips

Once you could sail right across Brittany via the Nantes-Brest canal, an ambitious project initiated by Napoleon in 1810. The canal was completed twenty-six years later and principally used to carry coal and slate—a business killed stone dead by the First World War. The canal never recovered and the construction of a dam at Lac de Guerlédan in 1928 severed the link decisively. Now it is only possible to journey between Pontivy and Port de Carhaix by canoe.

Today the region's canals are rarely used by commercial traffic and pleasure boats have the run of these placid waterways. A speed

limit of only 3.7mph (6kmh) guarantees that any trip will be a leisurely progress through parts of Brittany few people see. Most boats and barges are hired well in advance by several holidaymakers for a week or fortnight but some companies will rent just for a day or weekend and some have boats that sleep

Mooring up at Dinan

only 2–4 persons. Bicycles can often be hired at the same time and a deposit (1,500F for example) is normally required.

Get in touch with a company direct and as early as possible—your chances of finding what you want will increase considerably if you avoid the peak months (August especially) but remember that many sections of canal close for works between mid-October and March. For more information contact the Comité de Promotion Touristique des Canaux Bretons, Office du Tourisme, place du Parlement, 35600 Redon.

There are four main sections of canal you can navigate, all part of a larger network of inland waterways. In Finistère this is along the River Aulne from Châteaulin to Port de Carhaix. Châteauneuf-du-Faou is the main centre; contact Argoat Plaisance, Port de Plaisance, BP 41, 29520 Châteauneuf-du-Faou. Tel: 98 81 72 11.

In Morbihan a canal runs along the River Blavet connecting Hennebont to Pontivy. This links Lorient to the Nantes-Brest Canal which runs from Pontivy to Redon to Nantes. Boats and barges can be hired from Le Ray Loisirs, 14 rue de Caradec, 56120 Josselin, Tel: 97 75 60 98, and Rohan Plaisance, BP 19, 56580 Rohan, Tel: 97 38 98 66. In Redon, from Comptoir Nautique de Redon, 2 Quai Surcouf, 35605 Redon, Tel: 99 71 46 03, and Bretagne Plaisance, Quai Jean-Bart, 35600 Redon, Tel: 99 72 15 80.

Another canalized section, the Canal d'Ille-et-Rance, runs between Dinan and Rennes with a connection south along the River Vilaine to Redon. Boats can be hired from Blue Line Bretagne, Argoat Nautic, Port de Betton, 35830 Betton, Tel: 99 55 70 36, and, near St Malo, Chemins Nautiques Bretons, Port de Lyvet, La-Vicomté-sur-Rance, 22690 Pleudihen, Tel: 96 83 28 71.

Nantes-Brest canal

Walking is the best way to discover Brittany. Some time during your visit you should abandon the car and take yourself off down one of the region's many well-signposted coastal tracks, forest trails and canal-side towpaths. As Brittany has no mountains to speak of few of these routes are arduous, most are well signposted and mapped and all let you escape into the relaxing peace of the Breton countryside.

Long-Distance Paths

France is criss-crossed by a network of long-distance trails known as *Sentiers de Grandes Randonnées* (GR). These are well-marked with red and white dashes and you could easily join one for a short walk or a day's hike. In Brittany no less than 21 GRs pass through, most of them following east-west inland routes. In the north GR34 runs from Fougères to Morlaix, in central Brittany GR37 weaves from Montfort to Douarnenez via Josselin and Huelgoat, and in the south GR38 runs from Redon to Douarnenez via Châteauneuf-du-Faou and Quimper. GR380 tours the Monts d'Arrée and the parish *closes* and GR341 connects Paimpol and Pontivy. GRs are well-mapped in the Topo-guides that detail their routes—in Brittany these are sold in local bookshops or they can be ordered from the Fédération Française de la Randonnée Pédestre, Centre d'Information, 64 rue

de Gergovie, 75014 Paris. Robertson-McCarta's *Walking Through Brittany* (See *Further Reading*) covers many of these routes.

Coastal Paths

Some of the GR routes touch the Breton coast, most notably the GR34 that follows the sea all the way from Mont St Michel to Morlaix. You could spend a pleasant day walking from St Malo to Cancale via Rothéneuf following this route, or take in a portion of the 55-mile (90-km) section that runs from St Brieuc to Lannion and covers the Côte de Granit Rose. Robertson-McCarta's *Coastal Walks:*

Normandy and Brittany can help you with these. Some walks follow the old coastguards' footpaths (*Sentiers de Douaniers*) which skirt the cliffs and coves, for example the well-trodden path that runs from the oyster-beds of Cancale out to the Pointe de Grouin, the 'Watchpath Walk' from Le Val-André to Port Dahouët, the *sentier* from Perros-Guirec to Ploumanach and the coastguard path that runs the length of Belle-Ile's Côte Sauvage.

Sentiers de Pays

Feeding into these long-distance and coastal paths are numerous *Sentiers de Pays* (country trails), often radiating from inland hiking centres like Huelgoat and Paimpont. They offer good and easy walking with the routes often described in companion guides to local *Petites Randonnées* (PR) available from bookstores and Tourist centres. Some longer routes are known as *Grandes Randonnées de Pays* and marked with yellow and red dashes, like that which tours the Pays Gallo to the west of Dinan. Further details on these can be found in a booklet *Randonnée Info* (in French) available from La Maison de la Randonnée, 9 rue des Portes Mordelaises, Rennes 35000.

Long-distance trail

Country trail

Towpath Walks

If you like an easy level walk you might care to take in some of the 900 miles (1500km) of towpaths (*chemins de halage*) that accompany Brittany's extensive network of inland waterways. GR37 follows part of the Nantes-Brest canal and is probably the most useful route. Further information from: Comité de Promotion Touristique des Canaux Bretons, Office du Tourisme, place du Parlement, 35600 Redon.

Huelgoat and the Parc Régional D'Armorique (Itinerary 3)

Tucked into the south-eastern corner of the Monts d'Arrée, Huelgoat is a lakeside resort well placed both for easy walks in the surrounding forests and boulder-strewn valleys and for hikes around the Parc Régional d'Armorique.

In Huelgoat look for the Café du Chaos at the eastern end of the lake where a path leads you down into the valley of the River Argent. Here enormous rocks carpeted with moss have created a series of sylvan grottoes—further east there are wooded walks out to Camp d'Arthus, once an important Roman fort, or you can follow a canal, built in the 18th century to serve nearby lead and silver mines, round towards Le Gouffre. Further details from the Tourist Office in Huelgoat, which is in a small square just off the main street, rue des Cendres.

Huelgoat and its forests

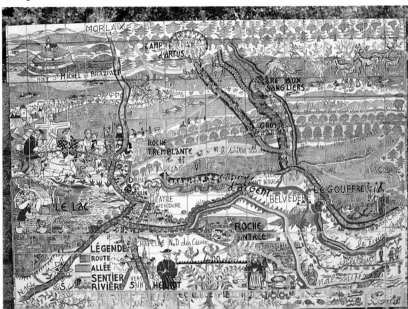

Valley of the River Argent

Mur-de-Bretagne and the Forêt de Quénécan (Itinerary 4)

Mur-de-Bretagne lies at the eastern end of the Forêt de Quénécan, close to the man-made Lac de Guerlédan and the Nantes-Brest canal. The area calls itself the *Coeur de Bretagne* and it's an excellent base for walking, camping, riding, boating, fishing and watersports. There are two very useful sources of information on what you can do here: the Pavillon du Tourisme in the centre of Mur-de-Bretagne and a smaller office next to the 12th-century Abbaye de Bon Repos, just south of the N164 at the western end of the Lac.

Well-marked trails

Walkers should consider following part of the GR341 path that skirts the shores of Lac de Guerlédan, or visit the two smaller lakes, Lac de Fourneau and Lac des Salles. You can also buy booklets detailing *Petites Randonnées* in the area, or take a stroll down the tree-lined tow-paths that run beside the canal—Gouarec is a good starting point. To the north of the N164 there is undulating heathland with steep gorges at Gorges du Doulas (up the D44) and Gorges du Toul Goulic (both on the GR341), and further west at Gorges du Corong.

Paimpont and the Forêt de Brocéliande (Itinerary 5)

Paimpont stands at the centre of the Forêt de Brocéliande, a bewitching remnant of the dense primeval forests that once covered the Argoat. It's one of the many places King Arthur and his knights are believed to have visited in their search for the Holy Grail, and a legendary home of the sorcerer Merlin and the enchantress Viviane. Today Paimpont and its tangled forest is home to a thriving King

Arthur industry which has many serious and bearded devotees. Even if you have little time for such mysticism the forest is at least a magical place to explore.

The Forêt covers some 1730 acres (700ha), much of it still privately owned. Parts of it are far from ancient, being replanted with pines, but others are thick with mature beeches and oaks and a bright undergrowth of ferns. In the autumn of 1990 forest fires, following on from the devastation caused by the hurricane of 1987, blackened much of its arboreal chaos.

The Tourist Office in Paimpont can provide you with information on walking in the forest along with a map of the 'Circuit Brocéliande' you can follow by car. You'll find it confusing and probably get lost, but then you are trying to discover the secrets of a spell-bound forest. Both the Château de Trécesson, where Merlin is said to be entombed in stone (not open to the public) and the Château de Comper, home of the lake-obsessed Viviane (park open to public) are easily found. So is the church at Tréhorenteuc where some post-war wall-paintings achieve a rare marriage of Arthurian and Christian iconography. Not far from the church you can take a signposted walk to the steep-sided Vallée-sans-Retour and a rock where Morgane le Fay seduces false lovers.

You will also probably want to find Brocéliande's own Holy Grail, the elusive Fontaine de Barenton. This is the magic spring where Merlin first met Viviane. To get there take the D141 north from Tréhorenteuc, turning right at an unmarked hamlet known, significantly, as Folle-Pensée—if you reach La Saudrais you've gone too far. Pass through the hamlet following the signs to Camping Barenton, looking for a clearing and car park to the left signposted Fontaine de Barenton. From here you walk deep into the woods following the white dots painted on the trees. At a dot-less crossroads of forest tracks continue straight on up the hill—eventually the track divides three ways where you turn left. Unfortunately all the signs in Brocéliande tend to get moved and defaced—perhaps by Merlin but more likely by the anti-social hippies living in its woods. If you see anyone disappearing into the trees carrying an empty Perrier bottle (the spring water is said to have therapeutic powers) don't hesitate to follow them!

Château de Trécesson

Moules à la marinière

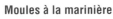

Regional Specialities

Brittany's menus rightly give pride of place to the superb fish and seafood harvested from the waters off its long coastline. Expensive luxuries elsewhere, you'll find that lobsters and oysters here are all affordable, fresh and served without fuss. Lobster *(homard)* cooked *à la Armoricaine* is often fêted as the region's premier speciality; the name, derived from the ancient Celtic word Armor, land of the sea, is often confused with the term *à la Américaine* though the result is the same—a sauce based on tomatoes, onions, herbs, wine and brandy. A simpler way to eat lobster is to just have it *grillé* (broiled).

Oysters *(huîtres)* are another famous Breton delicacy and Cancale is the place to eat them—see Option 2. Then there are clams *(palourdes,* or *praires* if they're small) and mussels *(moules,* also farmed on the north coast) which come either *à la marinière* (cooked in white wine with shallots) or *farcies* (stuffed). *Langoustes* are smaller, clawless members of the lobster family sometimes known as spiny lobsters or seawater crayfish—not to be confused with *langoustines,* which are large prawns (similar to Dublin Bay prawns) of which scampi is one type. There are also freshwater crayfish *(écrevisses),* shrimps *(crevettes),* scallops *(coquille Saint-Jacques)* and crabs—either the common *torteaux* or the flavoursome *araignées* (spider crabs). If you're feeling confused the best thing to do is to order a *plateau*

de fruits de mer (platter of seafood) soon after you arrive in Brittany and then spend the rest of your meal flagging down the waiter to ask *"Et quelle est cette créature étrange?"*

Brittany's fish are more straightforward: large quantities of cod *(cabillaud),* tuna *(thon,* often fried) and sardines are landed at its main ports while sole, plaice *(carrelet)* and turbot are often in the *poissonneries.* Monkfish *(lotte,* sometimes cooked in cider), sea bass *(loup de mer),* grey mullet

Oysters from Cancale

Experiences

Typical pâtisserie

(mulet), skate *(raie)* and eel *(anguille)* often feature on menus. *Soupe des poissons* is rarely disappointing while *cotriade,* a fish stew with onions, potatoes and herbs, is a Breton equivalent of *bouillabaisse.*

You'll probably find *à la bretonne* appears at least once on your menu: strictly speaking this is a garnish or sauce based on haricot beans, often served with lamb. Fish and eggs, however, can be served *à la bretonne* too and usually this refers to *sauce bretonne,* a cream-and-white-wine sauce with leeks. *Potée bretonne* is like a hot-pot, often made with lamb, sausage and vegetables. Dishes (scallops and white fish in particular) also come *à la nantaise* or with *beurre blanc,* terms which refer to a white wine sauce enriched by butter that is supposedly the creation of Nantes chefs.

For meat try some *gigôt* (leg) or *épaule* (shoulder) of *pré-salé* lamb *(agneau)* from the salt-meadows of Mont St Michel—grazed on pastures washed daily by the sea the lamb has a delicious (and expensive) ready salted flavour. Brittany is also a good excuse to treat yourself to some *chateaubriand,* named after the St. Malo-born author to whom this thick fillet steak (originally cooked with white wine, shallots and tarragon) was dedicated by the chef Montmireil. You could also try some *canard nantais*—duck from Nantes—while *dinde* (turkey) and *pintade* (guinea fowl) are often good value.

Vegetarians (save those who eat fish) are unlikely to be impressed by Breton cuisine. Vast tracts of Brittany may well be covered with nothing but vegetables but they never seem to make much of an appearance on the dining table; those that do—beans, cauliflowers, leeks, onions and artichokes in particular—are invariably delicious. Salads, often composed of a staggering variety of lettuces, are nearly always available.

Desserts are not especially Breton though you may see strawberries billed 'from Plougastel'. The cheese basket will require little research too—should you ask for *fromage breton* and get an affirmative response you'll probably be given something similar to Port Salut made by the nuns of Campenéac or some *fromage du Curé* (also called *nantais* and not unlike St Paulin or Pont l'Evêque) invented by a priest of the Vendée in the 19th century.

If you're having lunch you might prefer to skip the dessert and call in later at a *pâtisserie* to investigate the sugary world of Breton cakes. *Far breton* is a custardy Yorkshire pudding mined with prunes or raisins—it tastes better than this sounds but it's not as irresistible as *kouign amann,* a treacly puff pastry made with unthinkable amounts of butter. *Gâteau breton* is a catch-all term for what is sometimes a straightforward fruit cake, at others something similar to British lardy cake.

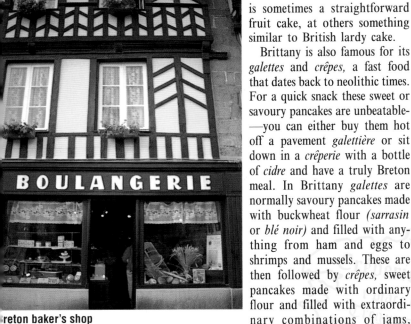

reton baker's shop

Brittany is also famous for its *galettes* and *crêpes,* a fast food that dates back to neolithic times. For a quick snack these sweet or savoury pancakes are unbeatable——you can either buy them hot off a pavement *galettière* or sit down in a *crêperie* with a bottle of *cidre* and have a truly Breton meal. In Brittany *galettes* are normally savoury pancakes made with buckwheat flour *(sarrasin* or *blé noir)* and filled with anything from ham and eggs to shrimps and mussels. These are then followed by *crêpes,* sweet pancakes made with ordinary flour and filled with extraordinary combinations of jams, syrups and ice cream.

Crêpes dentelles are 'lace' pancakes that originate from Quimper. They are like sweet rolled-up biscuits, crispy and thin: sometimes they're served with a dessert but you can also buy them in bakers and delicatessens. The term *galette* is also used to describe small shortbread biscuits made with butter—a Breton speciality that you can buy loose in *pâtisseries* or in packets in *supermarchés.*

Crêperie

Breakfast *(petit déjeuner)* is rarely included in the price of a hotel room and you shouldn't feel obliged to eat it there in the morning. It's quite acceptable (and often a lot cheaper) to wander off to a *boulangerie,* buy yourself a *pain chocolat* or some *croissants aux amandes,* then go to a café to eat them.

For lunch restaurants start filling up soon after noon and if you're not sitting down at a table by 2pm you could be in trouble. Lunch is still the main meal of the day for most Bretons, a leisurely affair that doesn't necessarily mean the consumption of vast amounts of food. In France you can order whatever you like how you like and a good restaurant will always accommodate the *caprices* of its clients.

In Brittany virtually all the restaurants offer two or three *menus à prix fixe* allowing you to select a choice of dishes for a fixed price. This doesn't include the price of drinks. You can also eat *à la carte,* generally more expensive and not always available late at night or at weekends. Eating out in France is still extremely good value—always investigate the *plat du jour;* as this is normally made from whatever's fresh and in season and may well be a Breton speciality.

For dinner restaurants open around 7pm and most people will be tucking in by 9pm. If you're out in the sticks don't leave it too late—if you spot somewhere you like the look of earlier in the day don't hesitate to reserve a table, particularly if it's for Sunday lunch. Restaurants close at least one day a week *(fermeture hebdomedaire),* sometimes on Sunday evenings, sometimes Mondays, but never all on the same day. If you're heading for somewhere special be sure to ring first and

97

Chouchen (mead), as drunk by Celtic deities

watch out too for the annual *congé* (holiday), particularly if you're visiting in September.

Choosing a restaurant in Brittany shouldn't be difficult. In this part of France hotels often provide the best fare around and you may well find you're most memorable meal comes not in a Michelin-fêted restaurant but at an unassuming two-star *Logis*. Recommendations for eating out have been included in the *Itineraries* and *Pick and Choose* sections, but if you like to digest a detailed review of a restaurant before you eat in it consult one of the many guide books written by the self-appointed restaurant buffs and assessors of French cuisine who regularly gorge their way across Brittany. See 'Further Reading' in the *Practical Information* section.

Simple food, but good

The Muscadet vineyards around Nantes may no longer be officially a part of Brittany but most Bretons continue to regard the wines they produce as a quintessential feature of the region's gastronomic pleasures. A crisp dry white wine with a high acidity, Muscadet is an ideal companion for the excellent seafood and fish caught off the Breton coast. One of the best-known is that from Sèvre-et-Maine; the expression *sur-lie* you often see on the label means that the wine has been matured on its lees (pips, skins) before being bottled, giving it a fruitier tang. Gros Plant, also from the Pays Nantais, is a coarser dry white, less expensive but with a less expansive taste.

Cider is the other principal Breton drink: that made from the apple trees around Fouesnant is the best though in northern Brittany you're more likely to be served the equally palatable cider from the Rance valley. It is considered the natural complement to *crêpes* but many Bretons drink it without food. Most *crêperies* will bring you the sparkling and corked *cidre bouché* but if you go to a *cidrerie* (cider house) you may well be served the locally made still cider—take care, it's often very strong.

Strawberry liqueurs

Beer is widely available—if you want draught ask for *un demi* (a small one) or *une bière a la pression,* for bottled *une bière en boteille.* Cervoise, the mystical brew of the Celts and strictly-speaking a barley beer, can be tracked down in trendy bars and delicatessens: it's dark and pow-erful and wisely comes both capped and corked.

Brittany, or rather the Rennes-based Jacques Fisselier label, also produces a range of regional liqueurs. None should sway you from wrapping up your meal with a *calvados* (apple brandy) from next door Normandy, but you may like to experiment with some of the miniatures sold everywhere. These include liqueurs made from local peaches *(pêche blanche),* blackberries *(mûre sauvage)* and Plougastel strawberries *(fraise).* There's also a cider-based *eau-de-vie,* a *whisky de Bretagne* and 'BZH', a Campari-like apéritif. More widely made is *chouchen* or *hydromel,* a mead born of fermented honey and water which tends to smell of honey rather than taste of it.

For coffee a small black one is simply *un café,* a large black *un grand café,* a small white *un crème* and a large white *un café au lait* or *un grand café crème.* Oh, and cheers is *Santé!*

Shopping

Shopping in Brittany is easy, enjoyable and inexpensive. One joy is discovering the pleasures of the region's specialities, another is visiting those traditional French establishments—the time-absorbing *caves,* the mouthwatering *charcuteries* and diet-destroying *pâtisseries*—that draw so many of us to France.

Shops in Brittany tend to open between 9 and 10am and then close again between noon and 1pm for a lunch break of at least two hours. They open again between 2 and 3pm, although in the country areas you'll find this can stretch towards 4pm. They then stay open till at least 6pm and often 7pm. In the resorts many will open longer hours during the summer season and in the cities some department and fashion stores stay open through the lunch hours—often called opening 'non-stop'. The majority of shops are closed on Sundays and Mondays, though some re-open on Monday afternoons.

Food shops such as *boulangeries* and *charcuteries* keep slightly different hours. These tend to open very early but take a longer lunch break, and there are usually one or two open on Sunday and Monday mornings. If you are planning a picnic be sure to buy everything before noon. Hypermarkets keep longer hours but are closed on Sundays.

Herbal remedies

Fish shop

Local Specialities

Honey, *pré-salé* lamb from the salt marshes of Mont St Michel, Breton cheeses, cider from the Rance valley or Fouesnant and Breton liqueurs are all good local buys. Look out for tins of Breton fish soup and seafood pâtes—the 'La Belle-Iloise' brand is made in Quiberon. Jars of home-made fish soup can also be bought in *poissonneries*. At the *boulangerie* look for *far breton, kouign amann, galettes* and *crêpes dentelles*. For more information on all these see *Eating Out*.

A rewarding purchase is a *crêpe*-making pan *(crêpière)* and all the necessary tools such as a rake *(râteau; rozell* in Breton) and a flat knife *(spatule; spanel* in Breton). Tell the sales assistant whether you will be using a gas or electric cooker and don't forget to buy some cider bowls and a jug to go with it.

For clothes Breton fishermen's sweaters, stripey matelot shirts and fishermens' caps are *de rigeur* buys. White duffle coats and wet weather sailing gear are good quality if you have need of them.

If you're heading for home beer, wine, coffee and cheese are notably cheaper in France. You can sometimes make savings on kitchenware too, such as Le Creuset pans and knives. Stationery is also reasonably priced. Tins of *galettes,* packets of ready-made *crêpes,* chocolate sardines and oysters all make economical and appropriate *cadeaux*.

Breton artichokes

Floral faïence

Handicrafts

Faïence is a distinctive hand-painted pottery that has been produced in Quimper for three centuries (see Option 6 in the *Pick 'n' Mix* section). Designs follow classical lines and often include blue and yellow borders with a decoration of flowers or animals. Plates and bowls are the most common purchases but mugs, cups and saucers and other crockery are available.

You'll find the widest selection in Quimper but *faïence* is sold throughout the region. There are also mass-produced imitations (the design is not fired into the pottery but painted on later) which are quite pleasant, considerably cheaper but not the real McCoy.

There is also a modern *faïence* produced by the Kéraluc factory with designs inspired by Brittany's Celtic heritage, as is the silver jewellery made by Toul Hoat. Wicker baskets are often sold in markets while *broderie bretonne* and lace is sold wherever large numbers of tourists gather.

For other local handicrafts Craft Fairs have the best and most original items—wood and granite are the favoured materials of local artists—and there is also a Breton Crafts Museum near Brasparts (see 'Museums' in the *Activities* section).

Breton lacework

Markets

Markets are one of the delights of France and no less so in Brittany. At the seaside they blush bright with seafood stalls run by ruddy-faced fisherwomen; inland you'll find the whole town turns out on *jour de marché* for a chinwag amongst the cheese and chainsaw stalls; in the cities it's all far more serious with green-grocers fussing over their displays like artists arranging a still life and *madames* in starched white aprons wrapping up your sausages as if they were Christmas presents.

Most markets are on only for the mornings, though in the larger cities like Quimper and Vannes some stallholders linger on well into the afternoon. In city centres like St Malo *intra-muros* or Vannes they can be split into different buildings a short walk from each other that will only sell, for example, fish, meat or flowers.

In the country markets they are often a jumble of stalls run by itinerant traders, an incongruous mix of live chickens and carving knives, berets and high-heeled *sabots*. If you don't set out to buy anything you'll undoubtedly find something of interest—keep an eye out for stalls selling local honey, *chouchen* (mead), cheese, wicker baskets and perhaps even some Breton records and tapes.

You may also encounter more specialist markets, perhaps selling livestock, crafts or *brocante* (antiques and second-hand goods). Fish auctions *(criées)* are a lively spectacle too: Concarneau's is the most famous and there are others of note in the ports at Roscoff, Audierne, Douarnenez and the southern ports of the Penmarch peninsula such as St Guenolé, Guilvinec, Lesconil and Loctudy. You'll need to get up early though so it's advisable to check first with the local Syndicat d'Initiative before you set the alarm!

Plenty of souvenirs

This is a guide to market days in the summer months.

Monday: Auray (fortnightly), Bénodet, Combourg, Concarneau, Douarnenez, Hédé, Ploërmel, Pontivy, St Quay-Portrieux, Trégastel, Vitré.

Tuesday: Étables-sur-Mer, Locmariaquer, Locronan (first in month only), Loctudy, Paimpol, Pont-Aven, St. Malo, St Pol-de-Léon, St. Servan, Trébeurden, La Trinité, Le Val-André.

Wednesday: Carnac, Paramé, St. Brieuc, Tréguier, Vannes.

Thursday: Carantec, Châteaulin, Dinan, Hennebont, Huelgoat (fortnightly), Lamballe, Lannion, Morlaix, Pont l'Abbé.

Friday: Auray, Concarneau, Douarnenez, La Trinité, Perros-Guirec, Quimperlé, St Brieuc, St Servan, St Malo, St Quay-Portrieux,

Saturday: Baud, Carhaix-Plouguer, Dol-de-Bretagne, Douarnenez, Guingamp, Josselin, Landernau, Paramé, St Brieuc, Vannes.

Sunday: Cancale, Carnac, Quimperlé.

Duty Free Allowances:

On 1 January 1993 the European single market came into force, which means that goods for EC-residents there are no restrictions on the movement of excise goods carried by travellers between member states for their own personal use. For alcoholic drinks and tobacco products 'minimum indicative levels' have been introduced to discourage commercial transactions. For those with strong arms, the levels for goods purchased in ordinary shops (duty-paid) are as follows:

Alcohol: 10 litres spirits and 20 litres fortified wines and 90 litres wine (not more than 60 litres sparkling) and 110 litres beer.

Tobacco: 800 cigarettes and 400 cigarillos and 200 cigars and 1kg pipe or hand-rolling tobacco.

Duty Free shops will continue to operate until 30 June 1999—allowances also apply to travellers to and from non-EC countries:

Alcohol: over 38.8 proof 1 litre or not over 38.8 proof 2 litres or fortified/sparkling wine 2 litres plus still table wine 2 litres.

Tobacco: 200 cigarettes or 100 cigarillos/50 cigars/250gms tobacco.

Châteaux, Gardens and Museums

Here are some historical attractions that are not included in the *Itineraries* and *Pick and Choose* sections but which could easily be incorporated into your travels.

Near St Malo:

ROTHÉNEUF: **Manoir de Limoeleu**. 15th-century home of Jacques Cartier. Open June–September, closed Monday and Tuesday.

BÉCHEREL (south of Dinan): **Château de Caradeuc**, so-called 'Versailles of Brittany' with magnificent classical park and views of the Rance valley. Open daily 1 March–15 September, 15 September–1 November afternoons only, rest of year Saturday and Sunday afternoons only.

COMBOURG: **Château de Combourg**, turreted castle and park, birthplace of Chateaubriand and the setting for his bizarre *Mémoires d'Outre-tombe*. Open April–October, closed Tuesdays. Château open 2–5.30pm, park 9am–noon, 2–5.30pm.

PLEUGUENEUC (south-east of Dinan): **Château de la Bourbonsais**, 16th-century château with gardens, kennels and zoo. Open daily 2–6pm all year.

Breton château

Museum of Fish, Concarneau

Near Roscoff:

St Vougay (near Plouzévédé): **Château de Kerjean**, Renaissance château with collection of Breton furniture and changing exhibitions. Open all year—in summer daily 10am–7pm.

Parc Régional D'Armorique:

Ménez-Meur, Hanvec: woodland estate with information about the Parc's work plus enclosures of local wild and farm animals and a **Breton Horse Museum**. Open June–September daily 10.30am–7pm, May 1.30–5.30pm closed Saturdays, rest of year Wednesdays and Sundays only 10.30am–noon, 1–6pm, closed January.

Moulins de Kerouat (near Commana): restored **watermills** and tannery—part of the Monts d'Arrée Ecology Museum. Open daily July–August 11am–7pm, rest of year 2–6pm closed Saturdays, closed November 1 to March 15.

Maison Cornec (near St.Rivoal): restored **17th-century debt-collector's house**, part of the Monts d'Arrée Ecology Museum. Open daily July–August 1–7pm, June and 1–15 September 2–6pm.

Moulin de Vergraon, Sizun: **Water, River and Fishing Museum**. Open daily 10.30am–7pm July–August, 10.30am–12.30pm, 1.30–5.30pm June and September, rest of year 2–5.30pm Sundays and Wednesdays only.

St. Hernot, south of Crozon: **Mineral Museum**. Open daily July–September 10.30am–7pm, June 10.30am–12.30pm, 2–7pm closed Saturdays, October–May 2–5.30pm closed Saturdays.

Trégarvan (near Plomodiern): **Breton Rural School Museum** housed in restored turn-of-the-century school. Open daily 21 April–12 May 2–6pm, 1 June–15 September 1.30–7pm otherwise Sundays only 2–6pm, closed November–March.

Scrignac (north west of Huelgoat): **Hunting Museum**. Open daily except Tuesdays June–September 10am–noon, 2–6pm.

Loqueffret: **Pilhaouerien Museum**, devoted to the rag-and-bone men of the Monts d'Arrée. Open 1 July–15 September 1.30–6.30pm closed Mondays.

Mont St Michel de Brasparts (near Brasparts): **Breton Craft Museum**. Open daily July–August 10am–12.30pm, 1.30–7pm, 16 March–30 June and September–December 10am–12.30pm, 2–6.30pm closed Tuesdays and Wednesdays.

Near Quimper:

St. Goazec (near Châteauneuf-du-Faou): **Château de Trevarez**, turn-of-the-century château with experimental farm, garden and forest park with signposted trails. Open April–June, September daily 11am–7pm (gardens 1–7pm), closed Tuesdays. July and August both open daily 11am–7pm. Rest of year open weekends and public holidays.

COMBRIT (near Bénodet): **Musée des Musique Mécanique**, idiosyncratic museum of mechanical musical instruments collected by a local enthusiast. Open May–September 2–7pm.

PONT L'ABBÉ: **Musée Bigouden**, traditional Breton costumes. Open June–September 10am–noon, 3–6.30pm, closed Sundays.

DOUARNENEZ: **Musée du Bateau**, historic boats and fishing with working boatyard. Open daily 10am–noon, 2–6pm.

Near Vannes:

ST MARCEL: **Musée Régional d'Histoire de l'Occupation et de Résistance en Bretagne**, museum dedicated to the local Resistance and life under Occupation. Open 10am–noon, 2–6pm all year, closed Tuesdays.

SARZEAU: **Château de Suscinio**, 13th-century castle badly damaged in the Revolution and currently being restored. Small **museum of Breton history**. Open April–September daily except Wednesday mornings 9.30am–noon, 2–7pm. Rest of year at odd times.

Thalassotherapy

The medicinal value of sea air, seawater and seaweed has long been known to the Bretons. Brittany now has 11 thalassotherapy centres offering revitalising health tonics and longer courses of treatment. Invigorating hose-downs, underwater massage in seawater jet-pools, skin cleansing with seaweed mud-packs are combined with the comforts of a smart hotel.

Most visitors will stay at a centre for at least a weekend but you can normally start treatment on any day. Always book well ahead and take any relevant medical records with you.

ST MALO: Les Thermes Marins, Grande Plage, 100 boulevard Hébert, BP 32, 35401 St Malo, Tel: 99 40 75 75. Open February–December.

DINARD: Thalassa Dinard, Avenue du Château Hébert, BP 70, 35802 Dinard Cedex, Tel: 99 82 78 10.

PERROS-GUIREC: Centre de Thalassothérapie de Perros-Guirec, boulevard Joseph Bihan, Plage de Trestraou. BP 50, 22700 Perros Guirec, Tel: 96 23 28 97. Now open March–September.

ROSCOFF: Clinique de Ker Léna, rue Victor Hugo, BP 73, 29681 Roscoff Cedex, Tel: 98 24 33 33. Open all year. Institut de Thalassothérapie Rockroum, BP 28, 29681 Roscoff Cedex, Tel: 98 29 20 00. Open 18 February–16 November.

DOUARNENEZ: Centre de Cure Marine de la Baie de Tréboul Douarnenez, 42 bis rue des Professeurs Curie, BP 4, 29100 Douarnenez, Tel: 98 74 09 59. Open all year.

QUIBERON: Institut de Thalassothérapie de Quiberon, BP 170, 56170 Quiberon, Tel: 97 50 20 00. Open February–December.

BELLE ILE: Castel Thalassa, 56360 Le Palais, Belle-Ile-en-Mer, Tel: 97 31 80 15. Open 15 February–15 December.

CARNAC: Centre de Thalassothérapie, Avenue de l'Atlantique, BP 100, 56343 Carnac Cedex, Tel: 97 52 53 54. Closed January.

VANNES: Institut de Thalassothérapie Louison Bobet, Port Crouesty, BP 53, 56640 Arzon, Tel: 97 53 90 90. Closed 1–15 December.

Nightlife

Brittany is not a place for night owls—come 10pm in a small country town you could easily find yourself the only person dancing in the high street. That said, the seaside resorts often work hard to provide their visitors with evening entertainment in the summer months. Casinos lead the way with those in St Malo (Esplanade St Vincent) and Dinard (Palais d'Émeraude) probably the most popular—you will need your passport.

All the resorts have at least one disco, but the quality does vary. In less seasonally minded cities such as Quimper or Vannes you'll find some bars and cafés have live music. If you do find yourself kicking your heels consider a trip to the cinema (many have a showing around 9pm) or try to catch one of Brittany's numerous festivals (see *Calendar of Special Events*).

Visitors to Brittany can pursue many of the genteel and some of the more insane sports that man has devised. If you have a particular appetite the quickest way to find out what facilities are available is to call into the local Tourist Office. For spectators there is also a busy calendar of tournaments, regattas and Grand Prix competitions throughout *la saison*. The following list is an inexhaustive guide to sports that make the most of the region's outstanding natural features.

Breton Sports

Your best chance to catch these is at one of the many Celtic-flavoured festivals that take place in the larger towns or cities—the Festival Interceltique held in Lorient every August is the biggest of these (see the *Calendar of Special Events*). They will often include a sports day featuring demonstrations or competitions—Breton wrestling (Ar Gouren) is the most popular, followed by numerous trials of strength such as tossing the caber, tug-of-war, discus throwing and *tire-bâton* where the contestants try to lift each other using a pole. The atmosphere is similar to the Highland Games you find in Scotland.

Breton wrestling (1895), by Paul Sérusier

Water Sport

The best beaches for windsurfing are those between Audierne and Concarneau but boards (*planches à voile*) and tuition are available from surfing centres all around the coast. The Pointe de la Torche, near Pont l'Abbé, is where the serious aquabats head for.

Water-skiing is available in many resorts—for a detailed list of

109

facilities contact the Ligue de Bretagne de Ski Nautique, BP 99, 49303 Cholet. Diving off the Breton coast offers remarkable opportunities like exploring the Er Lanic Cromlech in the Gulf of Morbihan—contact the Comité Régional Bretagne-Normandie de la Fédération Française d'Étude des Sports Marins, 78 rue Ferdinand Buisson, 44600 St Nazaire.

Sailing

The challenges and pleasures of yachting off the Breton coast draw thousands of sailors here each summer. A list of harbour facilities and yachting schools is available from the Comité Régional du Tourisme, 74 rue de Paris, Rennes Cedex, tel: 99 28 44 30. In most resorts pleasure craft can be hired.

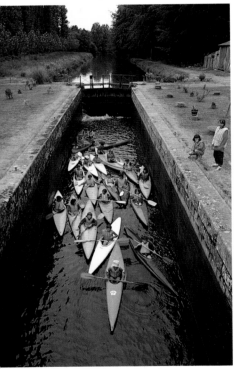
Canoeing, the Nantes-Brest canal

Sand yachts or buggies (*char à voile*) are a dry alternative ideally suited to Brittany's long hard sand beaches—for details of where these can be hired contact the Ligue Régionale de Char à Voile, 26 bis rue Belle-Fontaine, 56100 Lorient.

Canoeing

Intrepid canoeists who care to try sea kayaking should contact the Ligue de Bretagne de Canoë-Kayak, Ponthoën, Dervel, 22300 Lannion. For river and canal canoeing get in touch with the Association Bretonne des Relais et Itinéraires, 9 rue des Portes Mordelaises, 35000 Rennes.

Cycling

The French adore cycling and Brittany is no exception. Every Sunday its roads are illuminated by the bright jerseys of the cycling clubs out for a day's ride. If you want to join in each *département* has a local Comité Départemental de Cyclotourisme you can contact through its head Tourist Office (for addresses see *Practical Information*, pages 124-5). Most towns have cycle shops which will often hire you a bike for a few hours.

Sea fishing

Horse Riding

A rewarding way to get deep inside Brittany's countryside. Horses can be hired from many Centres Équestres, either by the hour or as part of an organised ride. Contact the Association Régionale du Tourisme Équestre en Bretagne, 8 rue de la Carrière, 56120 Josselin.

Angling

Sea fishing trips are available in some resorts, such as those from St Malo arranged by Emeraude Lines, and are often well advertised along quaysides. Fishing from the shore or a harbour wall can be rewarding if you have the right tackle and bait, and you are of course free to join the many Bretons who paddle around in the mud and rocks at low tide searching for prawns, shrimps and crabs. For river fishing it is necessary to join a local club (Association de Pêche et de Pisciculture) to get a licence—the staff of the local fishing tackle shop will usually help you in this matter. The banks of the River Aulne around Châteaulin are popular for trout and salmon fishing.

Golf

Brittany is currently enjoying a golfing boom and the region has numerous courses; the majority are on the coast with year-round facilities and at least 18 holes, although some of the older ones only have nine. Within easy range of St Malo you'll find courses at Dinard (Tel: 99 88 32 07), Sables d'Or-les-Pins (Tel: 96 41 42 57), Le Tronchet (Tel: 99 58 96 69) and also at Dol-de-Bretagne (Tel: 99 48 40 27).

Near Rennes there is a 9-hole course (Tel: 99 64 24 18) and the new 18-hole Golf de la Freslonnière (Tel: 99 60 84 09).

Further west you'll find Golf des Ajoncs d'Or at St Quay-Portrieux (Tel: 96 71 90 74) and Golf de St Samson at Plemeur Bodou (Tel: 96 23 87 34).

In Finistère there is a course near Landerneau (Tel: 98 85 16 17) and one further south within range of Quimper at Clohars Fouesnant (Tel: 98 54 87 88).

There are also courses in Morbihan near Auray (Tel: 97 56 85 18), at Baden (Tel: 97 57 18 96), St Gildas-du-Rhuys (Tel: 97 45 30 09) and on Belle-Ile (Tel: 97 31 64 65).

Calendar of Special Events

In Brittany the year's celebrations are marked by two quite different occasions: the serious acts of religious devotion known as *pardons* and the cultural fêtes inspired by the region's Celtic and Breton heritage. Sometimes the two meet—a *pardon* may well culminate in a fair with folk dancing and stalls selling *crêpes* and local specialities while a *fête* will often begin its festivities with a religious ceremony, like the blessing of the fishing nets that opens the Fête des Filets Bleu in Concarneau.

Pardons derive their name from the Catholic church's tradition of granting indulgences to their parishioners on Saint's Days in order that their sins might be pardoned. The ceremonies often include the taking of vows and the seeking of cures. Many of their rites have been observed annually since the 16th century, even earlier in some cases, and *pardons* have therefore preserved many features of Breton culture that might otherwise have died out. For this reason they are considered to be part of Brittany's tourist appeal, though if you are not a religious person you may feel your presence is intrusive.

Some *pardons,* like those at Ste Anne d'Auray, Ste Anne-la-Palud and Le Folgoët, attract thousands of pilgrims; others are smaller and may include the blessing of specific subjects such as lawyers, cattle, apple trees or even cars. Ceremonies generally commence with Mass and proceed to open-air services outside the church. The high point is a pious procession, sometimes candlelit, in which the devout, dressed in local costume and singing Breton hymns, walk through the fields and streets carrying banners, statues and relics. In the evening there is confession and vespers, after which the lay festivities commence.

Regular *pardon*-attenders say that the atmosphere and solemnity of these occasions

Festive Dinan

14 juillet · Locronan · FÊTE · Les Collines Bleues

varies considerably from place to place and year to year. If you manage to catch one you should at least see some *coiffés*, hear the Breton language and perhaps feel the force of the superstitious winds that have buffeted Brittany over the centuries.

If, however, all you want to see is some traditional Breton dress and folk dancing, to hear the sound of the *biniou* (bagpipe) and the *bombarde* (oboe), to drink cider and eat *crêpes* as you watch some Breton wrestling, then you may find Brittany's secular festivals more rewarding. Their objectives are simpler: to keep Breton folklore alive, foster the cultural links between the seven Celtic regions—Brittany, Ireland, Scotland, Wales, Cornwall, the Isle of Man and Galicia—and have a damn good time. Further information and an annual programme for these is available from the Fédération des Comités de Fêtes Folkloriques Bretonnes, 4 rue de la Ville Liard, 35800 St Briac-sur-Mer.

The following calendar is only a guide and you should check dates with the local Tourist Office before setting out. If possible go with someone who knows what's happening. On public holidays (*jours fériés*) some museums and tourist sights are open but most shops and all banks and businesses closed. If a holiday falls on a Thursday or Tuesday things are invariably closed on the Friday or Monday.

January/February

The French celebrate everything with a grand meal and the New Year is no exception. It is invariably seen in with fireworks and *crise de foie* (crisis of the liver) caused by generous alcohol consumption. Naturally the **1st**, Le Jour de l'An, is a public holiday.

March/April

Pâques is a serious religious celebration in Brittany and **Easter Sunday** and **Monday** are public holidays. **April Ist** is known as Poisson d'Avril, their equivalent of April Fool's Day.

Breton coiffé

May

The **1st**, Fête du Travail (Labour Day), is suitably marked by a day off work. The **8th** is a public holiday too, VE Day. **Ascension** (usually mid-May) is a public holiday and also the day of St Herbot's *pardon*. On the **second Sunday** there is a *pardon* at Quintin (near St. Brieuc) and on the **third Sunday** one in Tréguier to honour St Yves, patron saint of lawyers. During May St Brieuc hosts a festival of Breton folklore, Le Mai Breton, with a *pardon* on the last weekend.

June

The Sunday and Monday of **La Pentecôte** (Whitsun) are public holidays (usually late May/early June). There is also a *pardon* at Moncontour (near Lamballe) and a Fête de Toulfouen (birds) at Quimperlé. The **following Sunday** there is a *pardon* at Rumengol, a traditional place of pilgrimage in the midst of the Forêt de Cranou. On the **23rd**, Midsummer's Eve, there is a *pardon* at St Jean du Doigt (near Morlaix) in which the village's prize relic, the index finger of St John the Baptist (brought here in 1437) is dipped in a basin to produce holy water. On the **last Sunday** there is a *pardon* at Le Faouet (near Quimperlé) while Carhaix-Plouguer honours its famous son, the warrior-linguist La Tour d'Auvergne, with a fête.

July

Either at the end of June or early in July the capital, Rennes, kicks off a heavy month of celebration with its ten-day Festival des Tombées de la Nuit, an energetic, city-wide celebration of Breton culture. On the coast St Brieuc hosts a festival of Breton music in early July. St Malo also stages a folkloric festival, Le Clos Poulet, in July and from mid-July to mid-August its annual Festival du Musique Sacrée.

On the **first Sunday** there is a major *pardon* at Guingamp and on the **second Sunday** a Fête des Brodeuses (embroidery) in Pont l'Abbé and a folkloric festival Ajoncs d'Or (golden gorse) in Lamballe. That day also marks Locronan's Troménie (also called the Fête des Collines Bleues), a hill-top pilgrimage in honour of St Ronan that follows the route to his hermitage. Every sixth year there is a larger scale Grand Troménie—the next is in 1995. The **14th**, Bastille Day, is an explosive public holiday marked by spectacular firework displays. Mid-July also finds Paimpol celebrating its fishing links with Newfoundland and Iceland with a colourful Fêtes des Terre-Nuevas.

On the **third Sunday** Fouesnant, set deep in the cider country south of Concarneau, holds its Fête des Pommiers (apple trees). In Douarnenez there is a Fête des Mouettes (seagulls). On the **25th** and **26th** one of the

Breton festivities, 1863

region's most famous *pardons* takes place, the Pardon of Ste Anne d'Auray (near Auray), mother of the Virgin Mary and patron saint of Brittany.

The week before the **last Sunday** in July Quimper holds its highly recommended Fêtes du Cornouaille, a week of Breton celebrations that attracts visitors and performers from all the Celtic nations and which culminates in a costumed procession through the city. On that Sunday there is a *pardon* on the Ile de Batz while that at Le Folgoët (north of Landerneau) in honour of St Christopher includes the blessing of motor cars. There is also a *pardon* in St Quay-Portrieux at the end of July.

August

On the **first Sunday** in Pont-Aven there is a Fête des Fleurs d'Ajoncs d'Or (golden gorse), started in 1905 by the poet Théodore Botrel who also wrote the well-known song 'La Paimpolaise'. There is also a *pardon* in Huelgoat the same day.

During the first fortnight of August an International Celtic Arts festival is held in Lorient, a lively cultural jamboree with stalls, shows and live music. In mid-August there are also Festivals of Breton Dance in Guingamp (La St Loup) and Châteauneuf-du-Faou and a *pardon* and Fête de la Mer in St Cast-le-Guildo (west of Dinard).

On the **second Sunday** St Briac-sur-Mer holds its Fête des Mouettes (seagulls) with Breton dancing, processions and nocturnal celebrations known as Fest-Noz. There is also Breton dancing in Douarnenez, a Fête des Bruyères (heather) in Beuzec-Cap-Sizun (near the Pointe du Raz), a Festival de la Mer in Plougasnou (north of Morlaix) and a Festival Folklorique des Genets d'Or (golden broom) in Bannalec (northwest of Quimperlé).

Mid-August is when Perros-Guirec holds its Fête des Hortensias (hydrangeas) while on the south coast the major resort of La Baule has a Grand *pardon* and a long weekend of Journées Culturelles Bretonnes. The **15th** is the Assumption of the Virgin Mary and a public holiday. In Plomodiern (north of Locronan) there is a Festival Folklorique du Ménez-Hom, in Vannes the Grande Fête d'Arvor, in Port Manech (south of Pont-Aven) a Fête de l'Aven and in Audierne (near the Pointe du Raz) a Fête d'Armor. There are also *pardons* in Moncontour (near Lamballe), Pont-Croix (near Audierne), Plougastel-Doulas (east of Brest) and Perros-Guirec.

The following Sunday there is a *pardon* in Rochefort-en-Terre (east of Vannes) and on the **third Sunday** Carnac holds its Grande Fête des Menhirs and Concarneau its spectacular fishermen's festival, the Fête des Filets Bleus. On the **last Sunday** there are *pardons* in Châteaunouf-du-Faou

(south-west of Carhaix-Plouguer) and at the Chapel of Ste Anne-la-Palud (north-west of Locronan), one of the best-attended in the Breton calendar.

September

On the **first Sunday** the *pardon* for Our Lady at Le Folgoët (north of Landerneau) is one of the greatest in Brittany. The church at Le Folgoët (Fool's Wood), built after a miraculous lily bearing the words 'Ave Maria' was found flowering above a simpleton's grave, has been a place of pilgrimage since the 15th century. There is also a *pardon* at Camaret. On the **8th** at Josselin there is a pardon in honour of Notre Dame du Roncier, also known as the 'Barker's Pardon' after three local children were cured of epilepsy at a festival in 1728.

On the **second Sunday** Carnac holds a cattle festival in honour of St Cornély. On the **third Sunday** there are *pardons* at Belz (west of Auray), Plouha (south of Paimpol) and Pontivy. On the **last Sunday** there is a Fête des Voeux (vows) at Hennebont (near Lorient) and at Pont l'Abbé a *pardon*. At the end of September or early in October Dinan stages its Fête des Remparts, a weekend of medieval frolics. On the **29th** there is a Michaelmas fair at St Brieuc.

October/November

All Saints' Day (Toussaint), the **1st**, is a public holiday, as is the **11th**, Armistice Day.

December

On the **4th** there is a pardon at Le Faouet. **Noël** (Christmas) is a traditional time for parties and cultural events and the **25th** is naturally celebrated with the grandest meal of the year.

What to Know!
Practical Information

TRAVEL ESSENTIALS

When to Visit

Brittany has a short and furious holiday season—providing you visit between April and October you can expect to find enough places open to keep yourself fed and sane. Nothing ever happens before Easter and it's often a month or so before they rev up the engines ready for the peak period, July and August. This ends abruptly with *la rentrée* (the end of the school holidays) and by mid-September you'll find the hatches are coming down.

This scenario only applies to the the seaside resorts and inland rural areas. In the cities and larger ports life rolls on with the museums and tourist attractions shortening their opening hours in the winter months. If you intend to tour around then late spring and early autumn are a good bet as roads and hotels are far less crowded and there's an odds on chance of good weather. If you're staying put July and August promise the warmest temperatures, but avoid travelling at the beginning of August when it seems as if France is trying to completely rearrange itself in a single weekend.

If you want to attend a *pardon* or one of Brittany's lively cultural festivals see *Calendar of Special Events*.

Climate

Brittany's weather is not unlike that of Britain's: unpredictable, broody, capable of glory. Summers are good when they happen, similar to those in southwest England but tending to last longer. Sunshine cannot always be guaranteed but warm temperatures can—on average 21°C (70°F) in July and August. Winters are only harsh on the west coast. It is often breezy, sometimes windy and the further south you go, the better the weather. Plan for rain and be pleasantly surprised.

Documents

All visitors require a valid passport. A British Visitor's passport (valid for one year) or a British Excursion Document (valid for trips up to 60hrs) can be obtained at Post Offices. Visitors from non-EC countries (including Canada, USA and Japan) do not require a visa if staying under three months—details can be obtained from your French consulate.

Electricity

220 volts. Sockets generally take round two pin plugs and most non-European appliances will need an adaptor.

Time Difference

For most of the year France is one hour ahead of GMT. French Summer Time runs from the last Sunday in March to the last Sunday in September.

Money Matters

Credit cards and Eurocheques are widely accepted, including in petrol stations and supermarkets. The best exchange rates are given by banks displaying a *Change* sign. Avoid changing money at hotels or bureaux which often charge a high commission.

Don't Forget...

Film, map, sunglasses, swimming costume and books. French hotels are notoriously mean with their towels and soap so take these along too.

HOW TO GET THERE

By Air

Flying to Brittany is ideal for business trips or for a short, impulsive break. If you plan to travel around try to arrange a fly/drive deal before you leave as car hire is expensive. There are a lot more flights in the summer months and not all connections are available in winter.

Brit Air fly from London Gatwick to Brest, Quimper and Rennes with cheap fares available if you travel at weekends. For details in the UK tel. 0293-502044, in France tel. 98 62 10 22, or any Air France agent. They also operate limited season flights from Cork to Brest and Nantes.

Air France fly from London Heathrow to Nantes, tel. 081-742 6600; in New York, tel. 212-247 0100.

Jersey European Airways fly from Bournemouth, Southampton and Exeter to Dinard via Jersey, and also from Guernsey to Dinard. For details in the UK tel. 0392-64440, in the Channel Islands tel. 0534-46111, in Dinard tel. 99 46 22 81.

It is also possible to fly to Paris and take an internal flight on to Brest, Quimper, Lorient, Rennes, or Nantes with **Air Inter**; details from Air France. In Paris contact Air Inter, tel. 45 46 60 60. You could also take the train (see 'By Train' below) and Air France and SNCF (French Railways) offer joint air/rail deals via Paris (details in London from Air France, tel. 081-571 1413; from Air France in New York tel. 212-247 0100).

By Sea

The main attraction of travelling to Brittany by sea is it allows you to take your own car, by far the easiest way to tour the region. Prices vary according to season and it is advisable to book well ahead if you plan to travel in the holiday periods. All the ferry companies offer inexpensive short break fares.

Brittany Ferries sail from Portsmouth to St Malo (9hrs) and from Plymouth to Roscoff (6hrs). They also sail from Cork to Roscoff. For details in the UK tel. 0705-827701 (Portsmouth) or tel. 0752-221321 (Plymouth); in Eire tel. CORK 277801; in France tel. 99 82 41 41 (St Malo) or tel. 98 29 28 28 (Roscoff).

Two companies with bases in St Malo operate ferry and hydrofoil services between the Channel Islands and St Malo and Dinard: **Emeraude Lines**,

tel. 99 40 48 40, and **Condor**, tel. 99 56 42 29. Condor also run a hydrofoil connection between Guernsey and Weymouth in summer thereby linking Weymouth to St Malo in a 5hr trip, for details tel. 0305-761551.

Another alternative is to take a ferry to Normandy and drive across to Brittany. **Brittany Ferries** have crossings from Portsmouth to Caen and from Poole to Cherbourg. **P&O European Ferries** sail from Portsmouth to Cherbourg and Le Havre, tel. 0304-203388. **Irish Ferries** also sail from Rosslare to Cherbourg and Le Havre, and in summer from Cork to Le Havre, tel. DUBLIN 61 05 11.

By Train

New high-speed (TGV) rail links have now cut the journey time between Paris and Rennes to only two hours, and to Brest to four hours. There are also fast connections from Paris to St Malo and along the south coast to Nantes and Quimper. For fares and times contact Continental & Rail Travel, 179 Picadilly, London W1V OBA, tel. 071-491 1573. In Paris tel. 45 65 60 60 for information. In the US contact the French Tourist Board. Brittany-bound trains leave from the Gare de Montparnasse—prior reservation is required if travelling on TGVs.

By Road

Rennes is 216 miles (348km) from Paris, Quimper 348 miles (561km). An *autoroute* (motorway with toll charges) runs from Paris virtually to the borders of Brittany. From there fast N roads penetrate the region along its northern and southern coasts. There are also good N roads to Brittany from the Channel ports in Normandy.

International coach operators offer services to Brittany by road via a cross-channel ferry to St Malo or Roscoff, details from Eurolines, tel. 071-730 0202.

Left, resort transport

If you want to see Brittany rather than France go west. Basse Bretagne, an area traditionally seen as lying west of an imaginary line running south from St Brieuc to Vannes, is where Breton culture is most evident. The north coast, particularly along the Côte d'Émeraude

and the Côte de Granit Rose, has the best beaches—wide and sweeping sands with room for everyone. The south is gentler, with wooded river valleys and a softer, sunnier ambience. The west coast is the most dramatic, rising to cliffs and rocky headlands buffeted by angry seas. Inland you'll find rolling farmland patched with ancient woods and man-made lakes, gentle rivers and rigid canals. In Finistère the land rises to moorland and the protected open spaces of the Armorica National Park. Then there are the islands, some flat and severe, others mild and bucolic.

For a short city-based break consider St Malo, Quimper or Vannes; for a *gîte*-based holiday pick an inland village within easy reach of the north coast beaches or one in the vicinity of the

River Odet. For a complete change consider the Ile d'Ouessant, for a complete rest Belle-Ile. Go to Carnac for mystery, the parish *closes* for history, Cancale for oysters and Quimper for pottery.

GETTING AROUND

The best way to see Brittany is by car and most people take their own vehicles over there by cross-channel ferry. Car hire is expensive in France but may be more practical for short trips. Public transport is efficient but not always convenient with rail routes favouring east-west journeys. Travelling by train and then hiring a bicycle at a local station is one possible solution. In such a relaxed landscape, cycling, walking, riding and river journeys are all viable alternatives.

Maps
Drivers should use Michelin route map No. 230 Bretagne or its smaller sections 58, 59 and 63, all 1:200,000. An alternative is the Red Series *carte touristique* 105 (1:250,000) published by the Institut Géographique National, the French equivalent of our Ordnance Survey. The Institut also publish a Green Series (1:100,000) which shows footpaths and a more detailed Orange Series (1:50,000) and Blue Series (1:25,000).

By Car
Brittany has no toll roads but has good dual carriageways (N roads) for fast journeys. The region is also fretted with quiet minor roads that invariably reward their explorers well. Petrol is more expensive than in the UK.

Drive on the right and take care—the roadsigns saying 'Speed kills, 71 dead in Morbihan since March' are not kidding. *Priorité à droite* is still a cause of confusion for many visiting motorists. *Priorité* still applies in built-up areas and you must give way to anyone coming from a side turning to the right, but it no longer applies to roundabouts and you must give way to cars already on them. Elsewhere all roads of significance outside built-up areas have right of way, marked *passage protégé*. Look out for signs such as *cedez le passage* and *vous n'avez pas la priorité* which both require you to give way as necessary.

Seatbelts must be worn by front seat travellers and motoring offences are often penalised with stiff on-the-spot fines. Speed limits are 130kph (80mph) on motorways, 110kph (68mph) on

dual carriageways, 90kph (56mph) on other roads and 60kph (37mph) in towns. Crash helmets must be worn by motor cyclists.

Car Hire
Car hire is expensive in France and it is best to arrange it before you leave through companies such as **Holiday Autos**, tel. 071-491 1111. Many airlines offer fly/drive deals and SNCF offer rail/drive packages.

By Taxi
Taxis can be hired in the cities and resorts from taxi ranks or called by telephone. If you are embarking on a long journey agree a price first.

By Bus and Coach
Bus services connect the parts of Brittany the trains don't. Most are run by private companies and their timeta-

bles designed to meet local needs rather than those of foreign travellers. SNCF also run useful bus services between their stations and nearby towns. Timetables are available from bus stations *(gares routière)* and Tourist Offices. Coach excursions to many of Brittany's sights, including special trips to see *pardons,* can be booked through travel agents, such as **Tourisme Verney** in St Malo (16 rue Auguste Fresnel, tel. 99 82 26 26) and **Castric Voyages** in Quimper (place de la Gare, tel. 98 56 33 03), as well as at some SNCF stations.

Driving

Drivers must be at least 18 years old and have a full driving licence. Fully comprehensive insurance is recommended. A green card is not compulsory but if you only have third party insurance it will give you more cover than would otherwise apply in France.

If you are taking your own car you must carry the vehicle registration document, insurance certificates and a letter of authorisation from the owner if it is not registered in your name. It is advisable to carry a red warning triangle, obligatory if you do not have hazard warning lights. You will also need a complete kit of spare light bulbs, headlamp-converters for right-hand drive and a GB sticker. Unleaded petrol *(essence sans plomb)* is widely available in France.

By Train

Brittany's railway lines provide good east-west connections with routes from Rennes along the northern coast to Brest and along the southern to Quimper. North-south travel is trickier but a link line connects these two termini and there is a good service from St Malo to Rennes. There are also lines from Guingamp to Carhaix and St Brieuc to Loudéac with SNCF buses continuing south.

Train services are efficient and bicycles can be hired from many stations. If you will be travelling a lot by rail consider getting a *France Vacances* Pass which allows unlimited rail travel in France for four days or longer. Discounts are also available for travellers under 26, families and senior citizens. Further information from French Railways, 179 Piccadilly, London W1V 0BA, tel. 071-491 1573.

By Bicycle

Cycling is an extremely pleasurable way to see Brittany. With a plethora of minor roads, cyclist-friendly motorists and a good supply of repair shops you can't go wrong. Bikes are carried free on cross-channel ferries and for a small fee on trains and buses. On most SNCF trains a bicycle has to go as registered luggage and a small fee is charged.

Bikes can also be hired by the day from most SNCF stations. For information on routes contact the Touring Department, Cyclists Touring Club, Cotterell House, 68 Meadrow, Godalming, Surrey GU7 3HS and the Association Bretonne des Relais et Itinéraires (ABRI), 9 rue des Portes Mordelaises, 35000 Rennes. Cycling

holidays are also available through companies such as Triskell Cycle Tours, tel. 0902 678255.

By Horse

Riding across Brittany is an attractive proposition. The region has a good stock of equestrian centres, some of its *gîtes d'etape* offer stabling and there are plenty of circuits and itineraries to follow. Hiring a *roulotte* or horse-drawn caravan is another possibility. For further details contact Cheval-Bretagne, Locmaria Berren, 29218 Huelgoat or the Centre Régionale du Tourisme Équestre (for address see *Sport*). Companies such as Leicester Study Groups, tel. 0509 231713 and the French organisation La Maison de la Randonnée, 9 Rue des Portes Mordelaises, Rennes 35000 offer organised riding holidays in Brittany.

By Boat

Brittany's inland waterways provide a leisurely way to see the region—see Option 11 in the *Pick and Choose* section.

By Foot

'Walking is virtue, tourism deadly sin' as Bruce Chatwin put it. See Option 12 in the *Pick and Choose* section.

WHERE TO STAY

Always book well ahead, something essential if you plan to visit Brittany in July or August. If you are touring it is well worth ringing a hotel in the morning to make a reservation—they will normally expect you to arrive by 6pm. Should you find everywhere full the Tourist Offices are usually very helpful.

Hotels

Hotels in France are graded from one- to four-star with prices quoted per room. The majority of those available in Brittany are two star with a room for two with bath costing around 250F per night. Breakfast is extra. Standards vary considerably but soft beds and orange wallpaper on the ceiling are a consistent feature. Some hotels have good restaurants but lousy rooms, others vice-versa. If you plan to do a lot of hotel-hopping you may find it useful to buy a specialist hotel and restaurant guide—see *Further Reading*. A booklet listing all Brittany's hotels and their facilities is available from the French Government Tourist Office.

It is normal to be shown a room and then asked if it is suitable: if it isn't don't hesitate to ask for another, perhaps for *une chambre avec vue* or *loin des bruits de la rue*. If you are only staying one night some hotels may ask you to agree to eat in their restaurant before they will grant you a room. This can become annoying and expensive but fortunately not all hotels have restaurants and they are often closed for at least one night a week.

Logis de France, an association of family-run hotels with a distinctive green and yellow logo, are invariably good value with pleasant rooms and friendly staff. There are over 300 *logis* and *auberges* in Brittany and a guide is available from the French Government Tourist Office in New York and London or from the Fédération Bretagne des Logis de France, 4 quai Ad. Thomas, 35260 Cancale. **Brittany Hotels** is another 45-strong chain of two-star hotels, details from Hôtel du Chateau, F-56120 Josselin, tel. 97 22 20 11. For something more luxurious try the **Relais et Chateaux** group, 9 avenue Marceau, 75116 Paris, for something

quiet **Relais du Silence**, 2 passage du Guesclin, F-75015 Paris, tel. 45 66 77 77. To stay on one of Brittany's islands contact **Ilôtels**, 45 rue Jean Jaurés, 56400 Auray, tel. 97 56 52 57.

Some hotels in Brittany can be booked through travel agents in the UK; these will also have details of the numerous companies offering short break packages there, such as **Brittany Direct Holidays**, tel. 081-641 6060. If you do contact a hotel direct you will probably have to send a deposit, perhaps using a Eurocheque. In Perros-Guirec, Quiberon and La Baule there are *Accueil de France* offices which will book hotels in the town up to eight days in advance for a small fee—personal callers only.

The following hotels are all good value: **Hôtel Les Voyageurs**, Berven,

29440 Plouzévédé, tel. 98 69 98 17. **Auberge St Thégonnec**, 6 place de la Marie, 29410 St Thégonnec, tel. 98 79 61 18. **Hôtel du Prieuré**, rue du Prieuré, Locronan, tel. 98 91 70 89. **Hôtel des Remparts**, 4 rue des Vierges, Vannes, tel. 97 54 11 90. **Le Relais Brocéliande**, 35380 Paimpont, tel. 99 07 81 07.

Other Accommodation

Chambres d'Hôtes are similar to our bed-and-breakfast but better. Prices are comparable to a two-star hotel but include breakfast. They tend to be in rural areas or on the outskirts of town and are a good way to meet Bretons. You can normally have an evening meal as well, which you may eat with the rest of family.

Local Tourist Offices can provide lists of **Chambres d'Hôtes** in their area and some are part of the Gîtes de France federation (see below). **Fermes-Auberges** offer a similar arrangement but are on working farms. You can also B&B in a Breton *château* or manor, contact Château Welcome, tel. 0491 578803.

Gîtes offer self-catering accommodation in holiday cottages and apartments for a week or more, almost always in inland rural areas. They often get

booked up months in advance. For a handbook and details contact Gîtes de France, 178 Piccadilly, London W1V 9DB, tel. 071-493 3480. **Gîtes d'Étape** are basic, dormitory-style local authority-owned hostels situated near walking, riding and cycling routes. They are open to all, unlike **Auberges de Jeunesse**, youth hostels, which are only open to members of the Youth Hostel Association; details from YHA, Trevelyan House, 8 St Stephen's Hill, St Albans, Herts. AL1 2DY, tel. 0727-55215.

Camping

Brittany is ideal for camping and has more sites than any other region of France. Most are near the coast and some are extremely sophisticated, more like canvas hotels where campers book in for a week or two's holiday. They are graded from one-to four-star and can get booked up in high season. For details and reservations of three-and four-star sites contact Camping Plus, 69 Westbourne Grove, London W2 4UJ, tel. 071-792 1944. There are also municipal sites, those on farms *(camping à la ferme)* and those called *aire naturelle de camping* which have minimal facilities.

USEFUL INFORMATION

Tourist Offices

Tourist offices are an invaluable source of information and help. In France they are known as Syndicats d'Initiative or Offices du Tourisme, and you will find then in most locations. They are normally open 10am–noon and 2–6pm.

In the UK contact the French Government Tourist Office, 178 Piccadilly, London WIV 0AL, tel. 071-491 7622. In New York at 610 5th Avenue, #222, New York NY 10020-2452, tel. 212-757 1125. In Brittany contact the Comité Régional du Tourisme, 74B rue de Paris, 35069 Rennes Cedex, tel. 99 28 44 30.

Each *département* also has its own head office: **Côtes d'Armor:** Comité Départemental du Tourisme, 29 rue des

Promenades, BP 4620, 22046 Saint-Brieuc Cedex, tel. 96 62 72 00. **Finistère:** Comité Départemental du Tourisme, 11 rue Théodore-Le-Hars, Bp 125, 29104 Quimper Cedex, tel. 98 53 09 00. **Ille-et-Villaine:** Comité Départemental du Tourisme, Préfecture, 1 rue Martenot, 35009 Rennes Cedex, tel. 99 02 97 43. **Morbihan:** Comité Départemental du Tourisme,

Préfecture, BP 400, 56009 Vannes Cedex, tel. 97 54 06 56.

Consulates

The American Embassy is at 2 avenue Gabriel, 75382 Paris, tel. 42 96 12 02. There are British Consulates at la Hulotte, 8 avenue de la Libération, 35800 Dinard, tel. 99 46 26 64 and at L'Aumarière, 44220 Couëron (Nantes), tel. 40 63 16 02 or in Paris at 9, avenue Hoche, 75008 Paris, tel. 42 66 38 10. There is also an Honorary Consul at 'La Hulotte', 8 avenue de la Libération, 35800 Dinard, tel. 99 46 26 64. In Paris the British Consulate is at 16 rue d'Anjou, 75008 Paris, tel. 42 66 91 42. The Irish Embassy is at 12 avenue Foch, 75116 Paris, tel. 45 00 20 87.

Tipping and Service

Most restaurants include service in their bills *(service compris)* but satisfied diners will often leave a tip as well. In bars and cafés it is customary to leave the waiter a few coins (at least 10 percent of the bill), and a similar amount should be given to hotel porters and taxi drivers, though tipping is not obli-

gatory. In bars you will normally pay a higher price for your drinks if you sit down at a table.

Facilities for the Disabled

Brittany is a viable summer holiday destination for disabled travellers. The proximity of the region, its beaches and invigorating sea air, its ready access to modern medical facilities and the possibility of thalassotherapeutic treatments are all positive attractions. Travel facilities are encouraging and Brittany Ferries and P&O offer free passage to the cars of registered disabled travellers. Most French railway stations have facilities for the disabled and local Tourist Offices will often provide free guides to the access, transport and accommodation available in their area.

There is also plenty of information available in the UK, though in the case of Brittany not all of it is up to date. The French Government Tourist Office can provide details of hotels in the area that make provisions for disabled guests, and a leaflet with addresses of French disability organisations that can help. For a good *resumé* of the information available, including holiday companies that cater for disabled travellers in Brittany, consult The Royal Association for Disability and Rehabilitation's annual handbook Holidays and Travel Abroad, available from RADAR, 25 Mortimer St, London W1N 8AB, tel. 071-637 5400. The charity Holiday Care Service also gives advice,

2 Old Bank Chambers, Station Road, Horley, Surrey RH6 9HW, tel. 0293 774535.

Children

Brittany is ideal for children. Not only does it offer safe family holidays by the sea and a good range of exhausting amusements and diversions, it actually likes them. Here children are not just tolerated but enjoyed, welcomed as guests in bars and restaurants.

Facilities for babies and children are good: nappies and powdered milk are widely available in supermarkets, most restaurants have high chairs and hotels can usually provide a cot *(lit bébé)* for a small

supplement. In the main resorts there are children's clubs on the beaches in July and August where for a small fee Junior can be deposited in a supervised bedlam. In restaurants children's portions can be ordered, or simply ask for another plate—invariably your child's food will come exquisitely presented and you'll secretly wish you could have ordered it yourself. However not all restaurants in Brittany are as welcoming as others (in some the poodles seem to get better treatment), so if your child has a monstrous tendency pick your establishment with care.

In France it is against the law for children under 10 to travel in the front seat of a car. On ferries and trains children under four travel free.

MEDIA & COMMUNICATION

Regional papers are widely read in France and Brittany's local paper *Ouest-France* has the largest circulation in the country. Some English newspapers are sold in the larger resorts and cities and it is often possible to pick up BBC radio broadcasts in Brittany.

Telephone

The French telephone system is good. Many public telephone boxes now take a phonecard *(télécarte),* minimum cost 50F, which can be bought from Post Offices, *tabacs* and newsagents. For long international calls you may find it easier to use one of the pay-at-the-end booths situated in or near main Post Offices. You can also telephone from bars and cafés but this may be more expensive, as it always is from hotels.

You only need to use a code if you are calling to or from Paris. To call Paris from Brittany the code is 16 then 1 then the eight figure number. To call Brittany from Paris the code is 16 then the eight figure number. Elsewhere (province to province or Paris to Paris) just dial the eight figure number.

To call Brittany from the UK dial 010 33 then the eight figure number. To call

Paris dial 010 33 1 then the eight figure number.

An engaged tone sounds like a rapid beeping. The operator is 13, Directory Enquiries 12. Calls are 50 percent cheaper between 10.30pm and 8am weekdays and from 2pm on Saturday onwards at weekends.

To dial other countries first dial the international access code 19, wait for the second bleep, then the country code: Australia (61); Germany (49); Italy (39); Japan (81); Netherlands (31); Spain (34); UK (44); US and Canada (1). If using a US credit phone card, dial the company's access number below: Sprint, Tel: 19 0087; AT&T, Tel: 19 0011; MCI, Tel: 19 00 19.

BUSINESS HOURS

Shops and Restaurants

Shops are generally open 9am–noon, 2–6.30 or 7.30pm, and closed on Sundays and Mondays. Food shops keep slightly longer hours—see *Shopping*. For restaurants see *Dining Experiences*.

Banks

Open 9am–noon, 2–4pm weekdays, closed Mondays. Remember to take your passport with you when cashing traveller's cheques.

Post Offices

Known as PTT or *Poste* and open at least 9am–noon, 2–5pm, 9am–noon Saturday in main towns. Stamps *(timbres)* can also be bought in a tobac-conists *(tabac)* and often wherever postcards are in sale. A postcard or letter to elsewhere in Europe costs 2.50F.

HEALTH & EMERGENCIES

EC visitors should take E111 form with you to France, available from main Post Offices in the UK. This entitles you to medical and dental treatment from the French health service, though you will have to pay for this first and then claim a refund back which will normally cover at least 75 percent of treatment costs and 40 percent of prescription charges. Refunds are paid by the local sickness insurance offices, known as *Caisses Primaire d'Assurance-Maladie,* so be sure to get the address of your nearest office before you leave.

If you are treated by a doctor or dentist show them your form straightaway to ensure they are *conventionée* (part of the scheme) and make sure you get a

feuille de soins (signed statement of treatment) before you leave. When you buy medicines at a pharmacist get the prescription attached to the *feuille de soins* as well as the *vignettes* (stamps) on the medicine containers. Everything is then sent to the *Caisse* for a refund. If you are hospitalized they will normally do all this for you but check first. Private medical or travel insurance is also a good idea.

For minor ailments you can visit a *pharmacie,* marked by a green cross, which is a good source of advice and devoted solely to the dispensing of medication. They will also be able to tell you where the nearest doctor *(médecin)* or dentist is.

Emergencies

For the Police or an Ambulance call 17, for the Fire Brigade 18. For medical emergencies in cities you can also call the Service d'Aide Medicale d'Urgence (SAMU) whose numbers are listed in the front of phone books.

Trouble

Brittany is generally a safe and law-abiding region and if you take the common sense precautions you normally would at home you should experience little trouble. As in all holiday resorts petty theft is a problem so don't invite it. Good travel insurance offers some consolation for any losses incurred.

FURTHER READING

For background reading the *Insight Guide: Brittany* offers in-depth essays on the region including a detailed history and articles on the Bretons and their culture; Per-Jakez Hélias' *The Horse of Pride* (Yale University Press) is a moving and autobiographical account of rural life in the pays Bigouden during this century. *La Route des Peintres de Cornouaille*, available in French or English from Tourist Offices and bookshops, is an excellent, well-illustrated guide to the region and its artists.

John Michell's *Megalithomania* (Thames and Hudson) is a lively survey of some of Europe's megalithic monuments and the people who have tried to explain them. Further historical insights are revealed in Pierre Abelard's *The Letters of Abelard and Héloise* (Penguin Classics), the confessions of an abbot stranded in Brittany in the 11th century, the *Selected Letters of Madame de Sévigné* (Penguin Classics), a view of

17th-century Brittany seen from a château near Vitré, and the *Mémoires d'Outre-Tombe* of René Chateaubriand (in French only), an entertaining chronicle of a late 18th- century childhood in a château at Combourg.

For fiction Honoré de Balzac's *The Chouans* (Penguin Classics) is an early romantic novel inspired by the Royalist uprising in Brittany that followed the French Revolution. Victor Hugo's *Ninety-Three* (Penguin Classics, currently out of print) covers similar ground while some of the action in Alexander Dumas' *The Three Musketeers* (Penguin Classics) takes place in Brittany.

The story of the Battle of the Thirty is retold in *Sir Nigel* by Sir Arthur Conan Doyle (Pan, currently out of print). Jean Genet's *Querelle of Brest* (Faber) is a lyrical low-life report from that port while Colette's *Ripening Seed* (Penguin), written in 1923, is a tender tale of adolescence and holiday romance set near Cancale.

The Ebony Tower by John Fowles (Pan) is a collection of stories inspired by Arthurian and Breton myths, with the title novella set in Paimpont forest. Nevil Shute's *Most Secret* (Pan) and Helen MacInnes's *Assignment in Brittany* (Fontana) are both World War II thrillers set in Brittany.

For hotel and restaurant guides Patricia Fenn's *French Entrée 5* (Quiller Press) offers diligent and witty reviews of establishments throughout Brittany. More general lists of recommended hotels and restaurants are available in guides covering all France by Michelin, Les Routiers and the AA. For something special consult *Staying in the Châteaux of Western France* by S and A Higgins (Roger Lascelles).

For walkers two of the Footpath of Europe Series published by Robertson McCarta are particularly relevant: *Coastal Walks—Normandy and Brittany* and *Walking through Brittany.*

ART/PHOTO CREDITS

The author and photographer would like to thank the following individuals and organisations for their help and assistance: Fuji Photo Film (UK) Ltd; Brittany Ferries Photo Library; Toby Oliver and Sarah Bensted-Smith at Brittany Ferries Information Bureau; Wendy Corfield at BCB; Pauline Hallam and Marc Humphries at the French Government Tourist Office; Sophie Goodfellow at the Brittany Chamber of Commerce; the Directors and Staff of the Comité Régional du Tourisme Bretagne and its numerous local Syndicats d'Initiative; Alice, Viv, Lilia and Claudia.

Additional photography cover, 3, 10/11, 21A, 25, 41, 62/63, 68, 81, 87, 93, 100, 105, 110, 113, 116, 119A, 123A, 126B	**Brittany Ferries Photo Library**
6/7	**D & J Heaton/Apa Photo Agency**
12, 13, 15, 36, 37B, 109, 114	**Editions Dufy**
21B, 22, 23, 24, 26, 27, 28, 32B, 33, 42B, 43, 48, 50, 55B, 61, 62A, 65, 66B, 70, 75, 76, 77B, 78, 79, 80, 81, 82, 83, 85, 88, 89, 90, 91, 94, 96, 97, 98B, 112, 113A, 118, 119B, 120, 122, 123B, 124B, 125A, 127	**Nigel Tisdall**
10	**Tony McCann**
Cover Design	**Klaus Geisler**
Cartography	**Berndtson & Berndtson**

Index

INSIGHT GUIDES

COLORSET NUMBERS

You'll find the colorset number on the spine of each Insight Guide.

INSIGHT *pocket* GUIDES

• •
United States: **Houghton Mifflin Company, Boston MA 02108**
Tel: (800) 2253362 Fax: (800) 4589501

Canada: **Thomas Allen & Son, 390 Steelcase Road East**
Markham, Ontario L3R 1G2
Tel: (416) 4759126 Fax: (416) 4756747

Great Britain: **GeoCenter UK, Hampshire RG22 4BJ**
Tel: (256) 817987 Fax: (256) 817988

Worldwide: **Höfer Communications Singapore 2262**
Tel: (65) 8612755 Fax: (65) 8616438

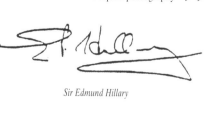

> **"** I was first drawn to the Insight Guides by the excellent "Nepal" volume. I can think of no book which so effectively captures the essence of a country. Out of these pages leaped the Nepal I know – the captivating charm of a people and their culture. I've since discovered and enjoyed the entire Insight Guide Series. Each volume deals with a country or city in the same sensitive depth, which is nowhere more evident than in the superb photography. **"**

Sir Edmund Hillary